James Barnor

Introduction by Christine Barthe

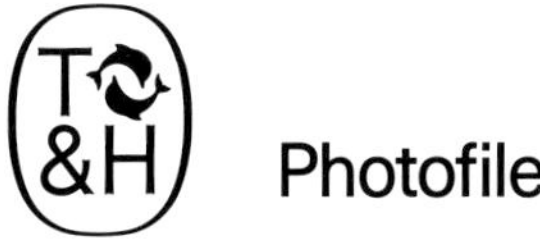

Photofile

Crossing Borders

It all started with a gift, a small camera, a Kodak Baby Brownie given to James Barnor in 1947 by one of his friends, Emmanuel Odonkor, a master weaver and fellow teacher at St Mary's Parish School in Accra, where James worked as an assistant to his friend and mentor, the art teacher A.Q.A. Archampong. This gift, which Barnor was given at the age of eighteen, marked a decisive moment, although it was not the only factor. In fact, James Barnor was surrounded by photographers, starting with his cousin J.P. Dodoo, who took him on as an apprentice. As a young man, Barnor worked at Yehowa Aakwe Studio from 1947 to 1949, but he was only allowed to learn by observing others at work and he later called his training 'strict'.[1] Then there was his uncle on his mother's side, William Ankrah, who ran a mobile studio in Accra and passed his photography equipment on to Barnor when he retired. This allowed James Barnor to set himself up as a studio photographer, at first shooting portraits outdoors: 'Whenever someone came, I asked them to go outside and hung up my backdrop.'[2]

The chance to have a more permanent base in the district of Jamestown opened up more opportunities for the young photographer, who founded the studio Ever Young in 1953. This space, which allowed him both to take photographs and to sell them afterwards, quickly became much more than a shop. It was a meeting place, a focal point where people gathered to socialize and play music, open day and night because it had electricity, which was still a rarity. Ever Young was a fashionable spot, a sort of community hub that stood out from the studios run by older photographers. Barnor's early portraits, taken in 1949–50, show his subjects in formal poses, either outdoors or against backdrops in J.P. Dodoo's studio, while his later images, from 1953 onwards, take a different approach, as the subjects began to adopt more casual poses and the atmosphere became visibly more relaxed. This is clear to see in the first portrait taken at Ever Young, a picture of a young female student simply sitting on the floor (ill. 3), and in photographs of Barnor's friends, such as Beatrice Okaijah, casually resting her elbows on a stool (ill. 5).

Another member of Barnor's family opened up unexpected opportunities for the young photographer: his cousin Julius Aikins, who in the late 1940s worked for the West African Photographic Service, a colonial photographic bureau. Through Aikins's connections, James Barnor discovered a number of photographic publications. This access to photography in books and magazines completed his practical training[3] and gave him a wealth of visual references to draw on. Even at this early stage of his career, he refused to be limited by a strict, pre-determined framework: 'With books and a small camera, you can go anywhere,'[4] he said. The window onto the world that he found in books, the international scope of the WAPS,[5] and the possibilities on show in the photographic press allowed him to diversify his practice. From the early days of his career, James Barnor combined many different approaches to photography. He practised street photography as well as traditional portraiture with a large-format camera against a backdrop, first outdoors, then indoors after he opened Ever Young in 1953.

The young photographer developed a love of motion and speed, which were made possible by using a small camera. His mentor J.P. Dodoo did not like these cameras, but James Barnor enjoyed using them and mastered them perfectly. In an interview with Margaux Lavernhe, he looked back on the 1950s, recalling: 'I had two lives. My first life, the life of the studio, where you stay still, and my second life, the life of the outside world, with the camera hanging from a strap, where you […] never stop moving. To do that, you have to know the people who count, open your eyes and ears to recognize what is going on.'[6] James Barnor always paid close attention to life, to movement, so he could sense when an event was about to take place: 'I went everywhere, wherever things were happening.'[7] It was because of this quality that J.P. Dodoo recommended him to the *Daily Graphic*, and he started working as a photojournalist for them in 1950. During this time, he witnessed the growth of anticolonial movements. In February 1951, he photographed Kwame Nkrumah, leader of the new Convention People's Party, on his release from prison (ill. 17). Nkrumah had been elected to government while he was still in prison for inciting civil disobedience. The following year, James

Barnor took a striking group photograph in which he himself appears, perching shyly on the arm of a sofa, alongside Nkrumah and the boxer Roy Ankrah (ill. 23). 1951 also saw the launch of Drum magazine, where James Barnor started working a year later. Founded in South Africa by Jim Bailey, the magazine was distributed in eight different countries across Africa, with its final issue published in 2000. Barnor's collaboration with Drum raised his international profile and proved useful during his time living in the UK in the 1960s.

The contacts that Barnor had made and maintained through his work and his studio, which gave him ample opportunities to meet new people, allowed him to avoid being pigeonholed by his ethnicity and social status. He was one of the first local photographers to be recruited by the Daily Graphic in 1950. The reason why he was granted accreditation to cover the celebrations marking Ghana's independence in 1957 was that he worked for a foreign agency: 'Local photographers had no chance because journalists from all around the world were in Ghana. It was only because I had been asked to represent a foreign agency that I was able to work there. I was treated like a foreign correspondent.'[8]

James Barnor knew how to surround himself with people he could trust. Thanks to Jim Bailey, he was present when Nkrumah declared Ghana's independence in 1957.[9] He turned to A.Q.A. Archampong for advice when trying to decide whether to move to London. When Archampong assured him that he could have a future there, James Barnor didn't hesitate, leaving Ghana for the UK in 1959. Although he was already a professional photographer and was familiar with many different styles, such as portraiture and reportage, his aim in moving to the UK was to continue his training. With a view to joining a new Ghanaian television channel in England, he studied at the London College of Printing, which allowed him to perfect his technical skills. On the advice of another mentor, Dennis Kemp, who worked for the Kodak Lecture Service, he decided to study at Medway College of Art in Rochester, Kent, from 1960 to 1963. He had happy memories of this period of his life, when he lived 'peacefully in a cocoon'. The training he received there was of a very high quality and he made friends with many other students. He added a number of new strings to his bow, learning techniques of applied photography, particularly advertising. In 1967, he started working for the Colour Processing Laboratory, which printed works by renowned photographers. This allowed him to master the latest techniques in colour photography.

James Barnor likes to tell stories. Just like the books he borrowed from Julius Aikins, his press work (first for the *Daily Graphic*, then *Drum*) attests to his affinity for storytelling and narrative: his photographs are all miniature stories. Throughout the 1960s, his ongoing work with *Drum*, including many covers for the magazine, brought him commercial opportunities, greater visibility and freedom, but it also meant his photographs were closely associated with journalism, image and text working together. The magazine had offices in London, which helped to ensure that Barnor consistently had commissions when he left Ghana: 'I felt at home in their offices on Fleet Street. Whenever I wanted something, they gave it to me.'[10]

Barnor worked with his models and friends Erlin Ibreck, Constance Mulondo, Rema Nelson, Marie Hallowi and Rosemarie 'Funflower' Thompson, creating urban images that revealed their subject's true character, transcending the genre of fashion photography and inventing a new, lively and joyful way of representing the African diaspora in the UK. These images, which have become emblematic of James Barnor's work, mark an important shift in his approach, probably because they stand at the crossroads between two practices that formerly had always been separate in Ghana: portraiture and street photography. James Barnor brought these two styles together, linking them closely to the network of friends and acquaintances that he was building at the time. The lack of dividing lines between his family, his network of friends and his photography was typical of the way he lived and worked, and was key to his success. In 1966, James Barnor brought along a young woman, a *Drum* model, when he was photographing Muhammad Ali in training for a fight against Brian London. She interviewed the boxer while Barnor took photographs, thus capturing Ali in action, in motion.

Another key trait of Barnor's is his readiness to take on new projects. His work with the Colour Processing Laboratory continued and he decided to introduce colour photography techniques to Ghana.

In the late 1960s, after a period spent training at the Agfa offices
in Germany, he returned to his homeland. In Accra, he became a
manager at Sick-Hagemeyer, a subdivision of Agfa in Ghana. Despite
a lack of support from the company's management, from 1970 to 1973,
James Barnor set out to establish a commercial colour photography
practice. It was during this time that he shot staged photographs
of himself and his colleagues posing with colourful containers and
pennants advertising the brand. Although the Agfa project did not last
long, the publicity shots that James Barnor took during this period
illustrate the new techniques that he would continue to draw on over
the years that followed.

Against a backdrop of both opportunities and constraints posed
by the unstable political situation in Ghana, in 1973 Barnor opened
a new studio in Accra, called X23, in the same district as Ever Young.
The images from those years use both black and white and colour,
with compositions that draw on the city setting: urban scenes full
of cars, with traditional African kente cloth featuring prominently.
Barnor also continued to portray his circle of friends, such as the
photographer Felicia Ansah Abban, who had opened her own studio
in Jamestown in 1953.[11] Barnor's portrait shows her posing elegantly
in front of Holy Trinity Cathedral (ill. 53). Some of the more intimate
portraits were taken indoors, combining spontaneous poses with
Barnor's mastery of light. Barnor also shot advertising campaigns,
notably for the brand Agip, using images that featured his family
(his daughter posing on a van) and his business (X23's branded car,
ill. 58) and drew on the aesthetics of fashion photography (an elegant
woman posing with oil cans, ill. 47) in the realist setting of the city
(with refineries and gas stations in the background). In both Accra
and London, cityscapes were a favourite setting for Barnor. He chose
a bustling, lively street, the one where Studio X23 was located, as the
backdrop for a portrait of the photographer N.T. Clerk[12] with a friend
in 1974 (ill. 52).

In the early 1980s, music began to play a bigger role in Barnor's
world. Urban settings remained important, and we can see Lutterodt
Street[13] in a number of the images he shot for record covers. Barnor
photographed groups such as The Happy Stars and The Youngsters

Band (ill. 68), as well as the musician E.K. Nyame (ill. 69), performing alongside street workers, always depicting Accra in a realist manner, making no attempt to dress up the setting. He also captured the young members of the Fee Hi cultural group walking out into the courtyard in front of Studio X23 (ill. 70). But from that point on, the photographer had to compete with other photographic technologies. After taking photographs for the US Embassy, from 1983 to 1987 he worked as an official photographer to the Ghanaian government, alongside his work at Studio X23, which remained open until 1992.

True to his habit of moving regularly between the two countries, James Barnor returned to the UK in 1994. After a few years, he settled in West London and a new phase of his life began, with his photographs starting to gain more recognition thanks to Autograph ABP. Founded in London in 1988 to promote the work of Black photographers, this organization publishes books and holds exhibitions. James Barnor's images began to be published and to circulate on the art market. The fact that he always carefully conserved his archives, prints, papers and negatives has become a key factor in the recognition he has enjoyed over the years that followed. Since 2016, he has been represented by the Galerie Clémentine de la Féronnière in Paris. He has gained greater visibility through a number of international exhibitions, including his first retrospective at the Nubuke Foundation in Accra in 2019. His French gallery is engaged on a project to digitize and create an inventory of the thousands of images that Barnor has preserved, working closely with the photographer himself. Little by little, names and dates are being filled in and the narrative thread is being reconstructed.

As has already been said, James Barnor likes to tell stories through his photographs. In this new stage of his career, he is fully involved with the creation of his archive, supplying valuable information about each image that only he can provide. His images become the basis for his narratives, the substance of his memories and the story of his many lives. For someone like Barnor, who places great importance on the idea of legacy, the opportunity to be involved in documenting his own work is nothing short of a dream. It is rare to have such a wealth of resources available: a rich body of work that comprises tens of thousands of images, the prodigious memory of their creator and his constant willingness to collaborate. Given his travels between Ghana and the UK, his work across diverse disciplines such as reportage and fashion photography, and his embracing of both studio settings and street scenes, some might view James Barnor as a restless figure in a state of permanent dissatisfaction, always seeking the new. However, the opposite is true: James Barnor is a man who values connections and legacy. His career and his photographs testify to his curiosity, his optimism and his trust in others. By exploring his work and restoring it to its context within the artist's life, it can be seen that the many paths James Barnor has taken in his life are undoubtedly connected to his photographs: those that he dreamed of, those that he created, and those that he has always been careful to keep with him.

Christine Barthe

Notes

1   'There was no syllabus. I studied the daily life of the studio, the work that was going on.' From Hans Ulrich Obrist, 'An interview with James Barnor', *James Barnor – Stories: Pictures from the Archive*, Bristol: RRB Photobooks and LUMA, 2022, p. 257.

2   Ibid., p. 258.

3   'Visiting Aikins at home, watching him work and looking through the books he recommended to me taught me so much.' *Ibid.*

4   Ibid., p. 261.

5   Margaux Lavernhe, 'Color is important, we have to start exporting color', *Photographica*, no. 3, October 2021.

6   Op. cit., p. 25.

7   Ibid., p. 261.

8   Ibid., p. 267.

9   Ibid.

10   Ibid., p. 268.

11   Erika Nimis, 'Felicia Ansah Abban', in Luce Lebart and Marie Robert, *A World History of Women Photographers*, London: Thames & Hudson, 2022, p. 310.

12   N.T. Clerk was a leading figure in Ghanaian photography, who notably photographed Prempeh II, 14th Asantehene (king of the Ashanti).

13   The Lutterodts were a family of photographers, active in Accra between 1870 and 1940. Many of James Barnor's photographs from the 1970s were taken in this street, because Studio X23 was situated a stone's throw away, on Asafoaste Nettey Road.

1. Portrait, Accra, c. 1950–51.

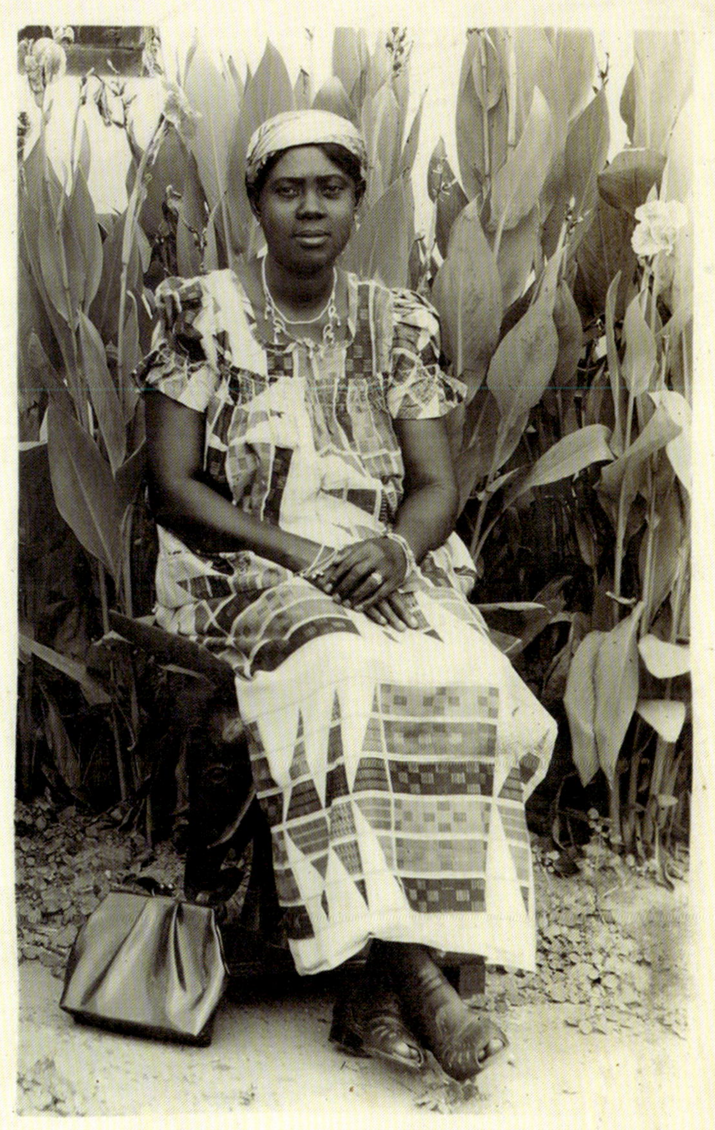

'EVER YOUNG' STUDIO
ACCRA

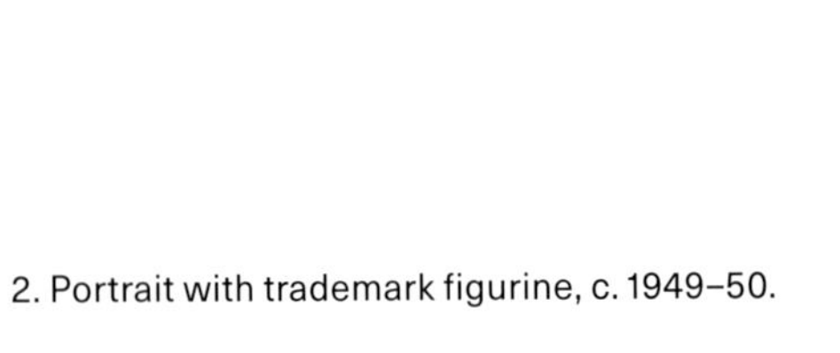

2. Portrait with trademark figurine, c. 1949–50.

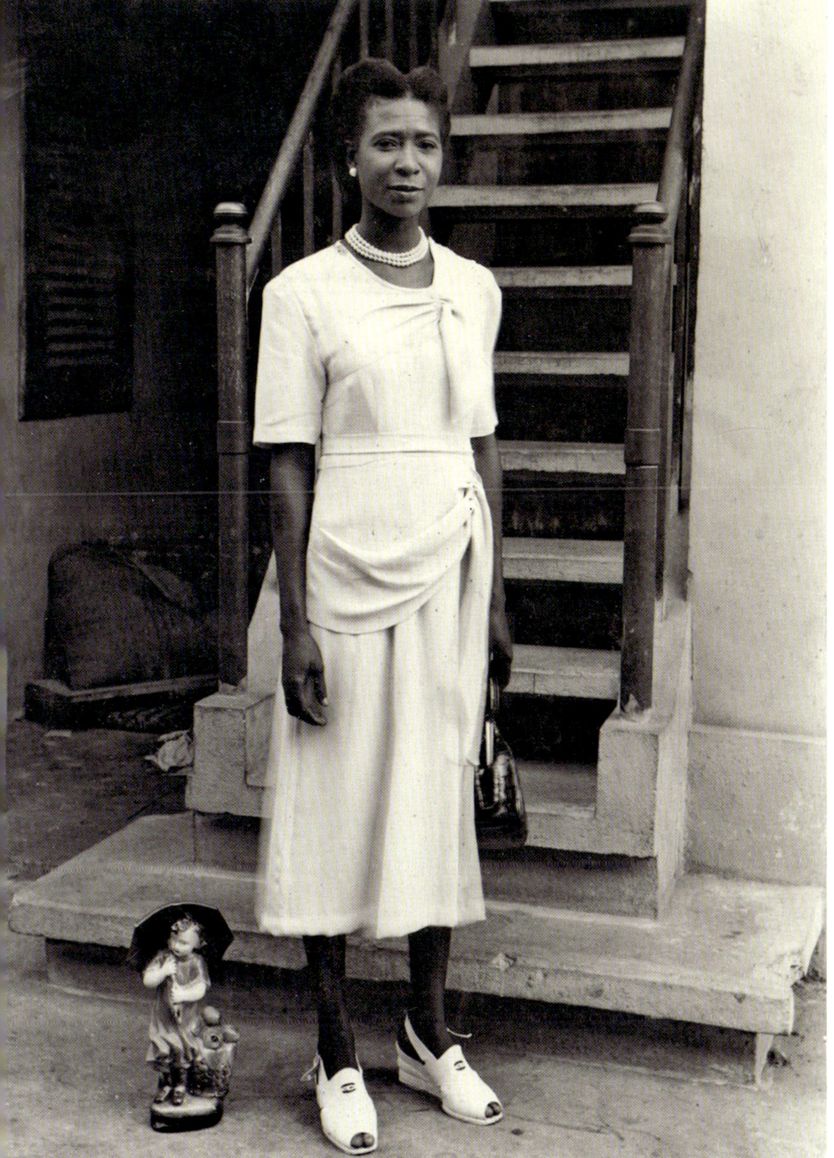

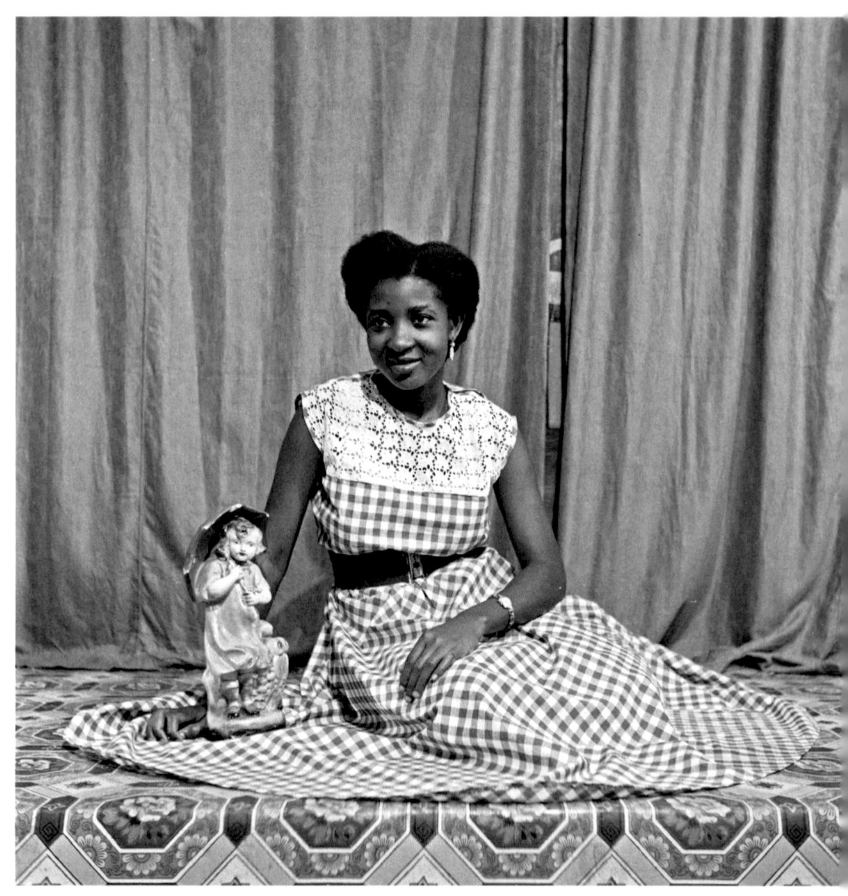

3. First portrait taken at the Ever Young studio,
Jamestown, Accra, 1953.

4. A.Q.A. Archampong, also known as Joy,
Ever Young studio, Jamestown, Accra, c. 1957.

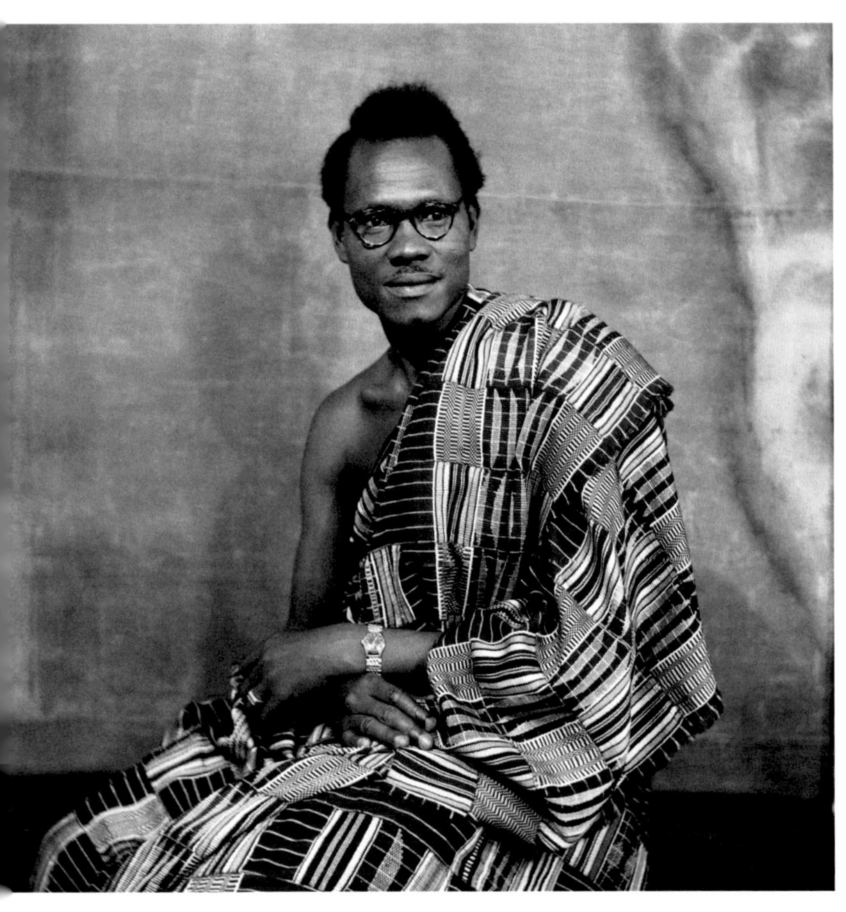

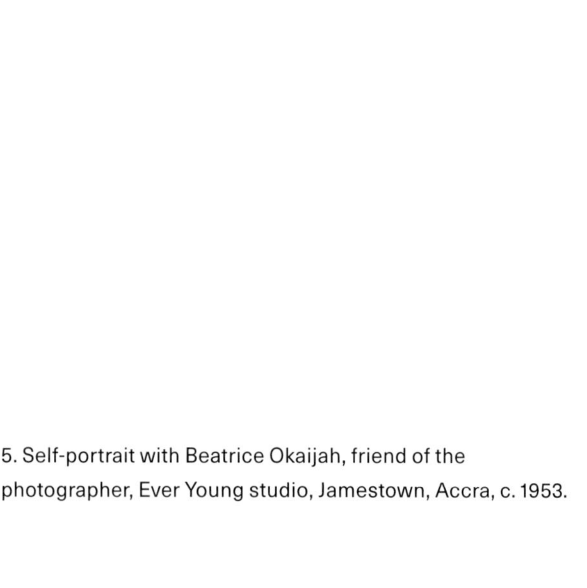

5. Self-portrait with Beatrice Okaijah, friend of the
photographer, Ever Young studio, Jamestown, Accra, c. 1953.

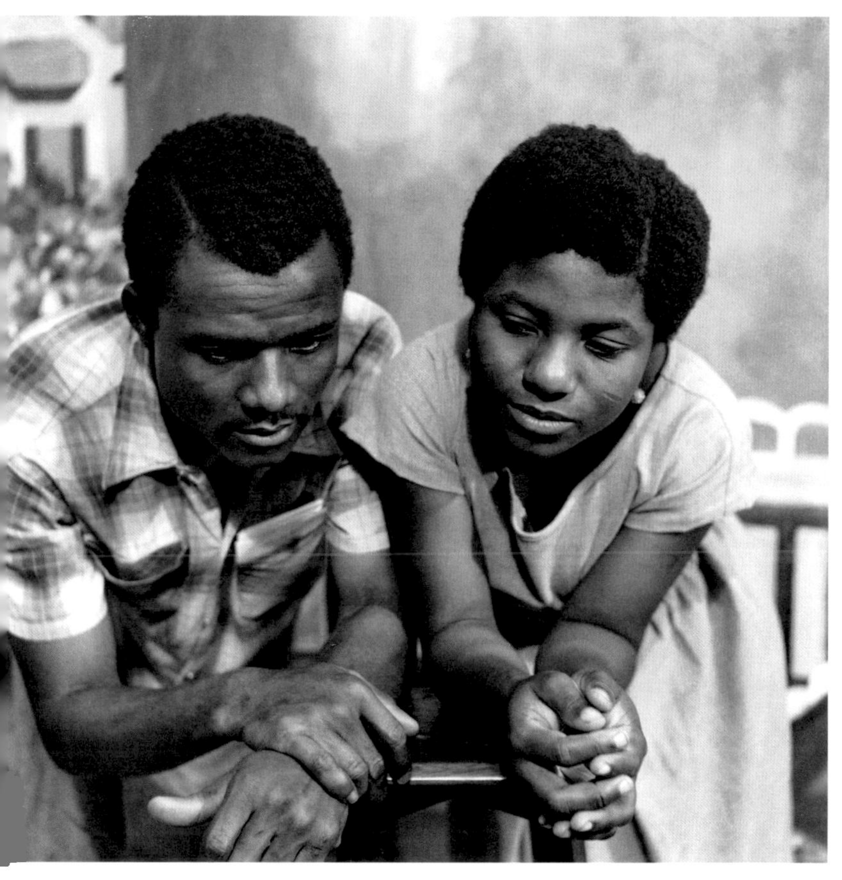

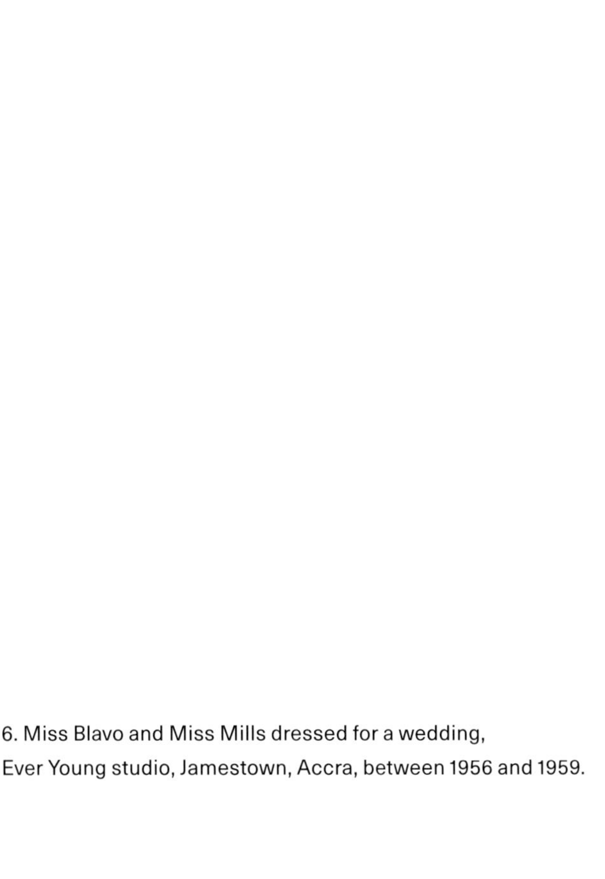

6. Miss Blavo and Miss Mills dressed for a wedding,
Ever Young studio, Jamestown, Accra, between 1956 and 1959.

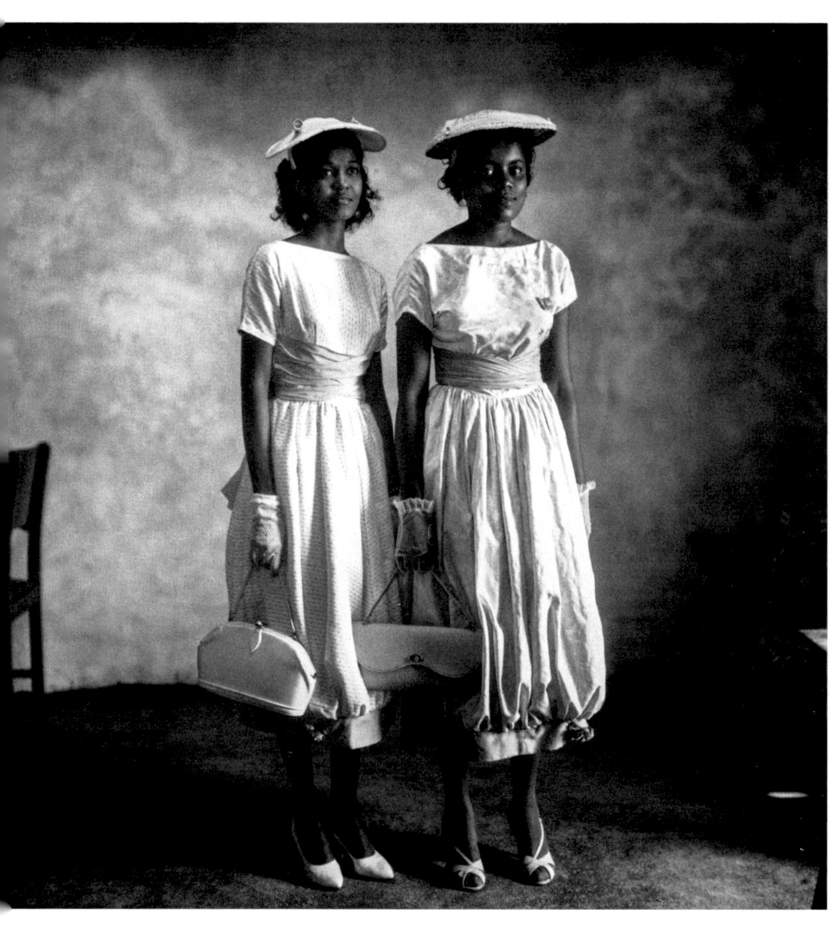

7. Evelyn Abbew, Sackey Mensah and a friend,
Ever Young studio, Jamestown, Accra, c. 1954–56.

Overleaf:
8. Ever Young studio, Jamestown, Accra, 1953.

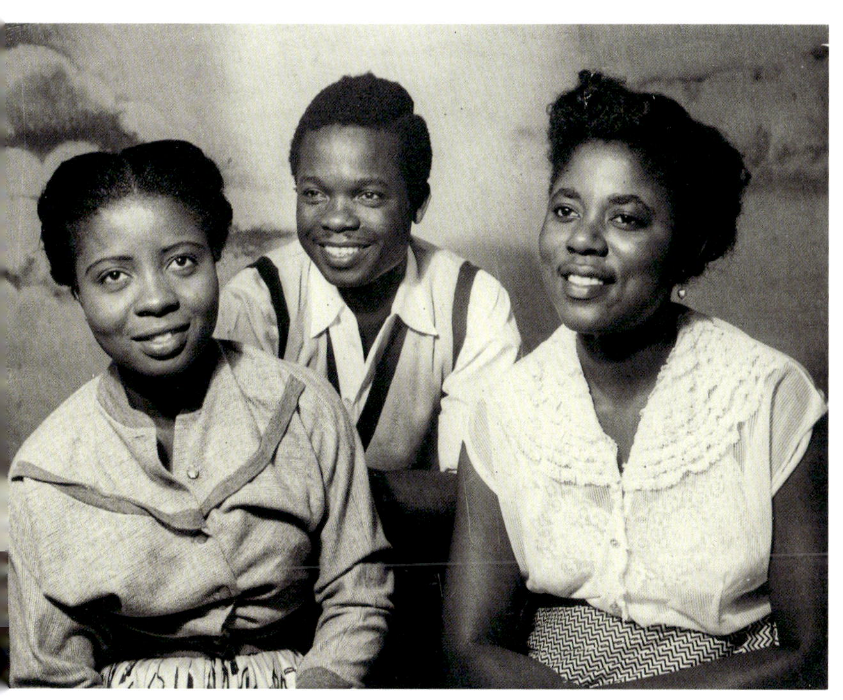

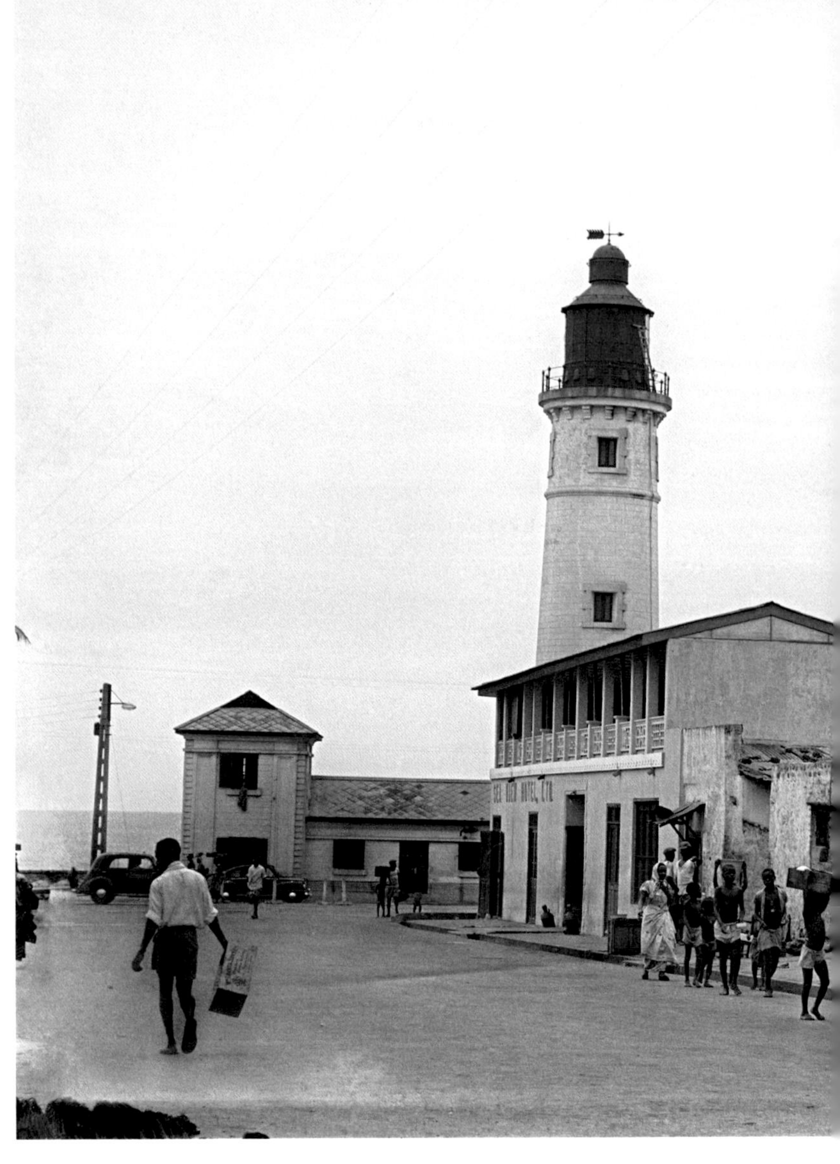

SEA VIEW HOTEL, LTD.

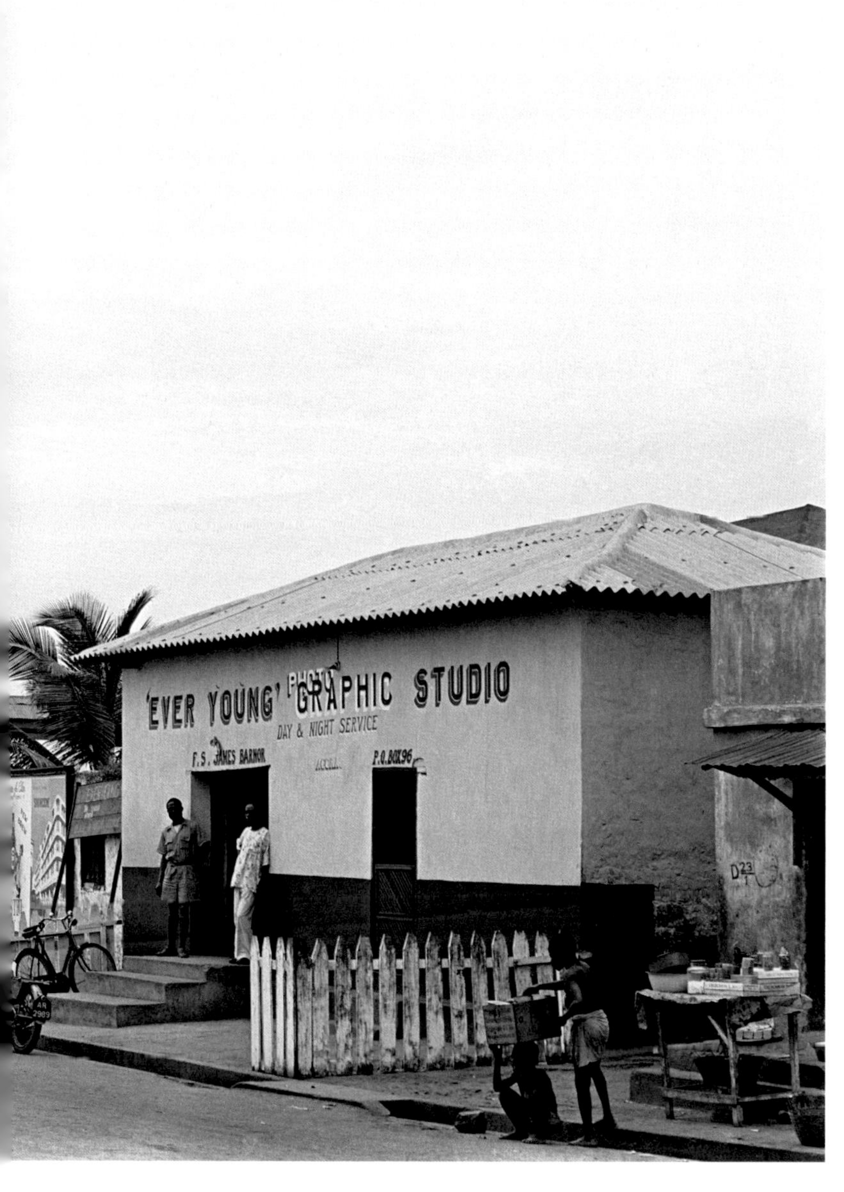
'EVER YOUNG' PHOTO GRAPHIC STUDIO
DAY & NIGHT SERVICE
F.S. JAMES BARNOR
ACCRA
P.O. BOX 96
D23

9. Self-portrait with Daniel Barnor, eldest son of James,
in the first travelling studio, Arena, Accra, 1952.

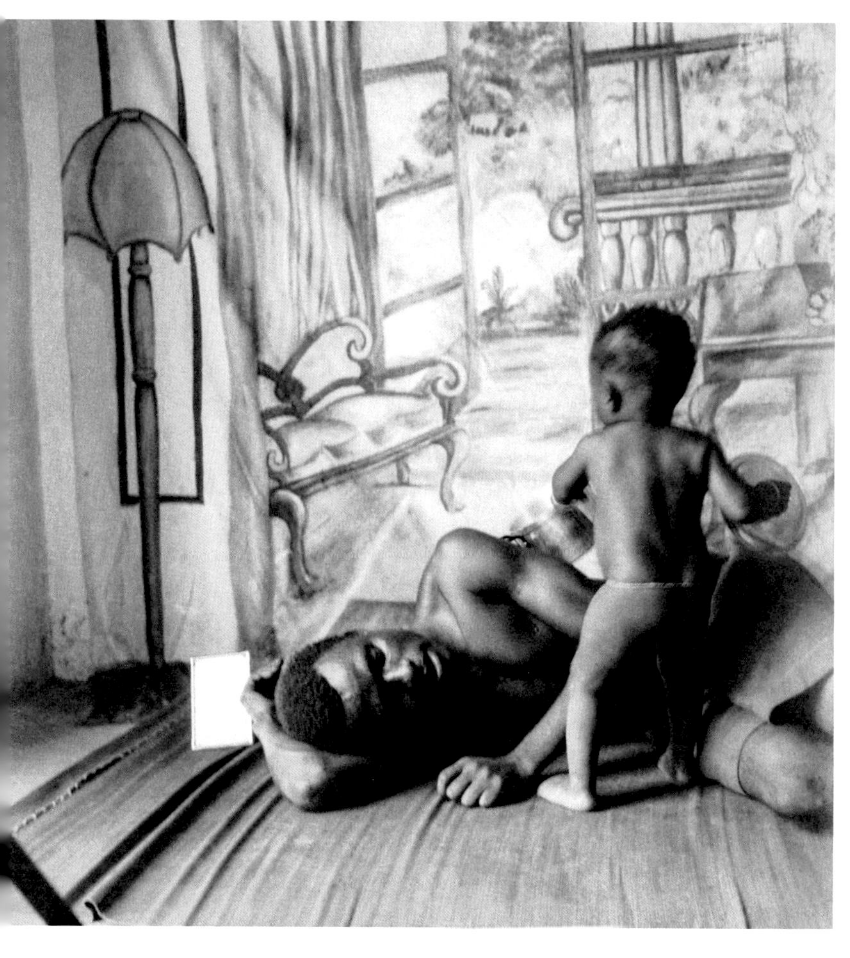

10. Julius Aikins in front of James Barnor's first studio, when he came to show him his Linhof camera, Arena, Accra, early 1950s.

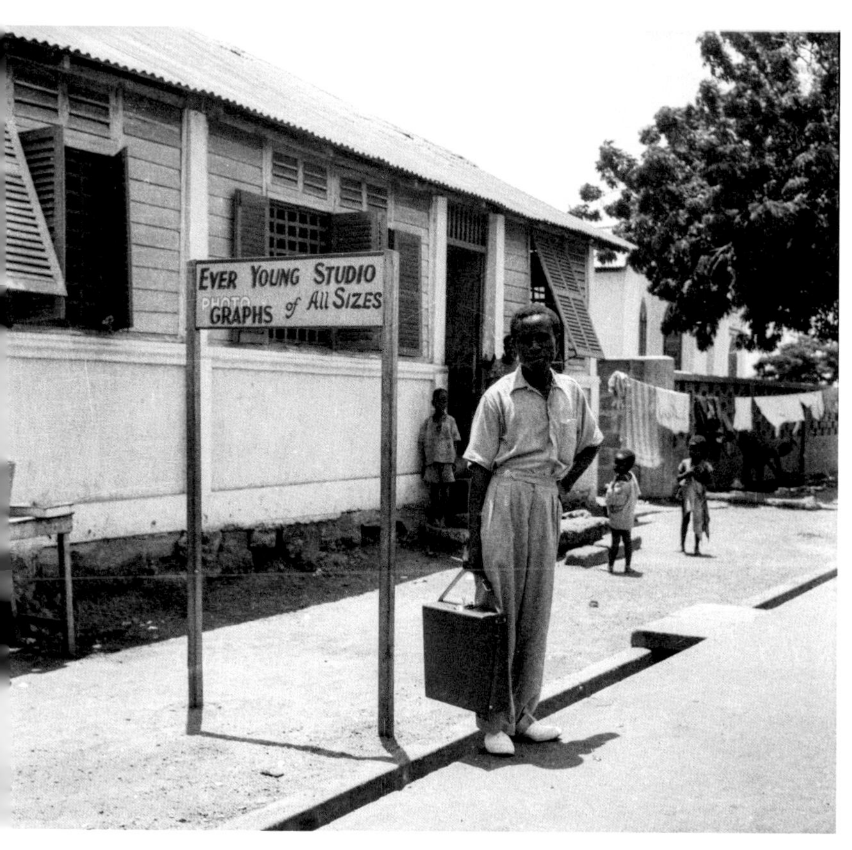
EVER YOUNG STUDIO
PHOTO
GRAPHS of All SIZES

11. Roy Ankrah during training, Accra, 1951.

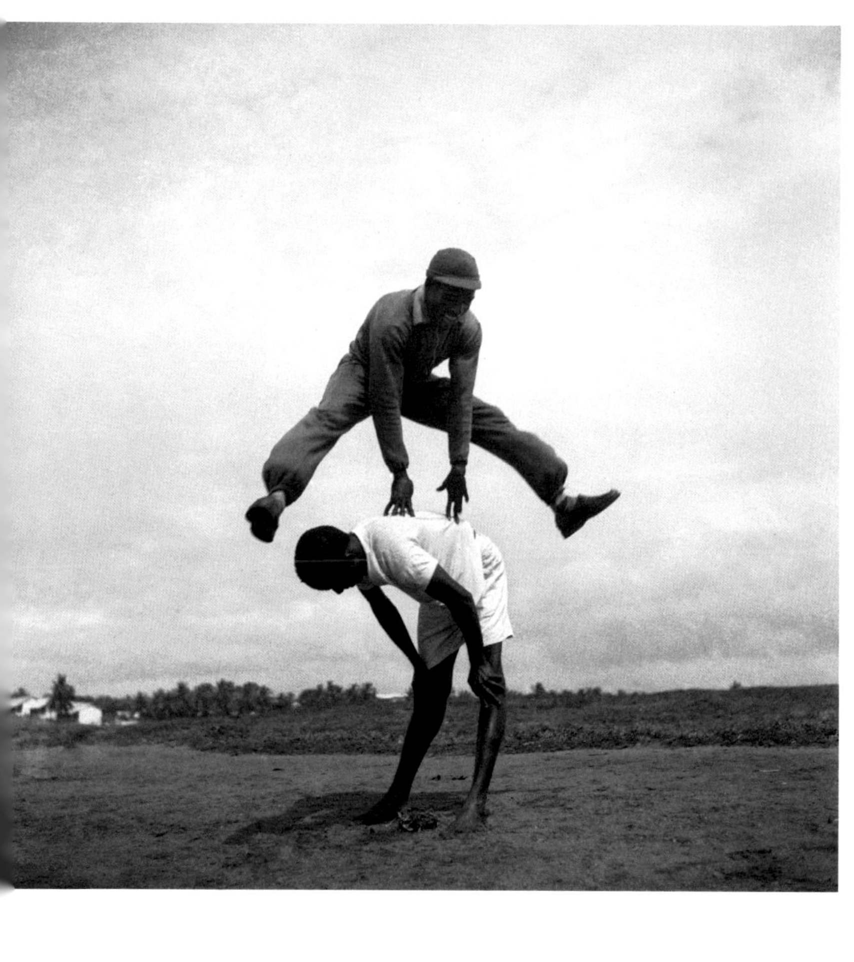

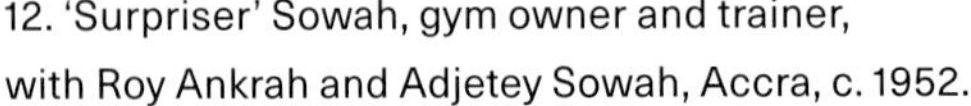

12. 'Surpriser' Sowah, gym owner and trainer,
with Roy Ankrah and Adjetey Sowah, Accra, c. 1952.

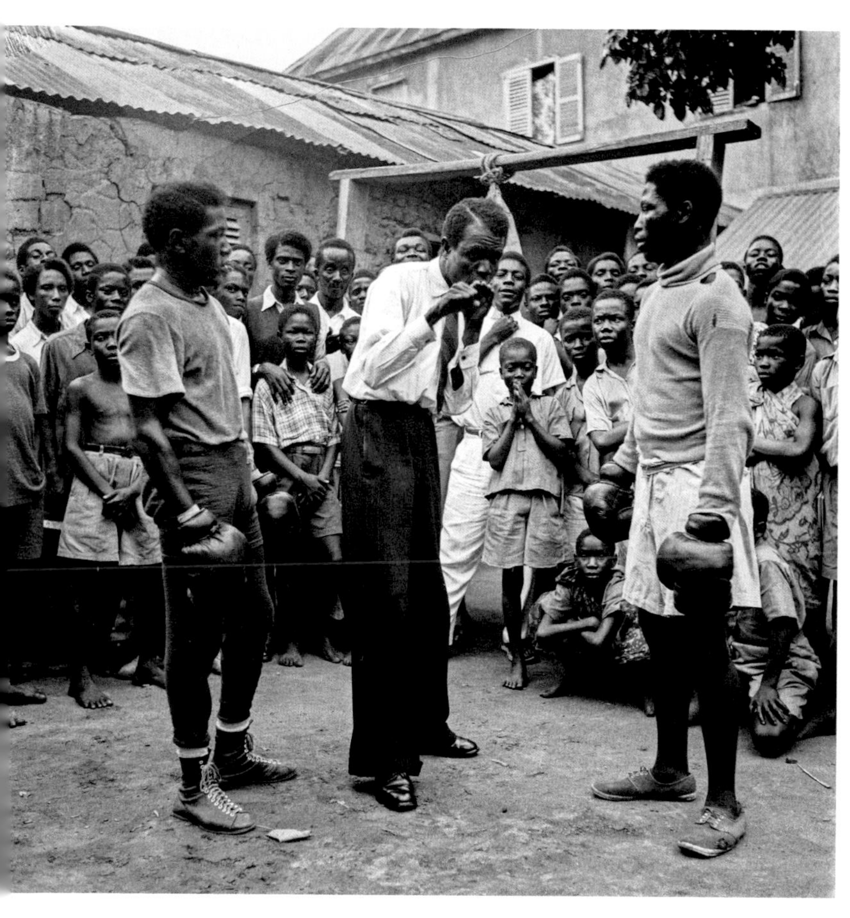

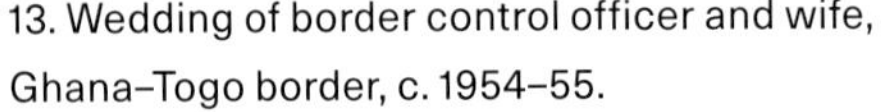

13. Wedding of border control officer and wife,
Ghana–Togo border, c. 1954–55.

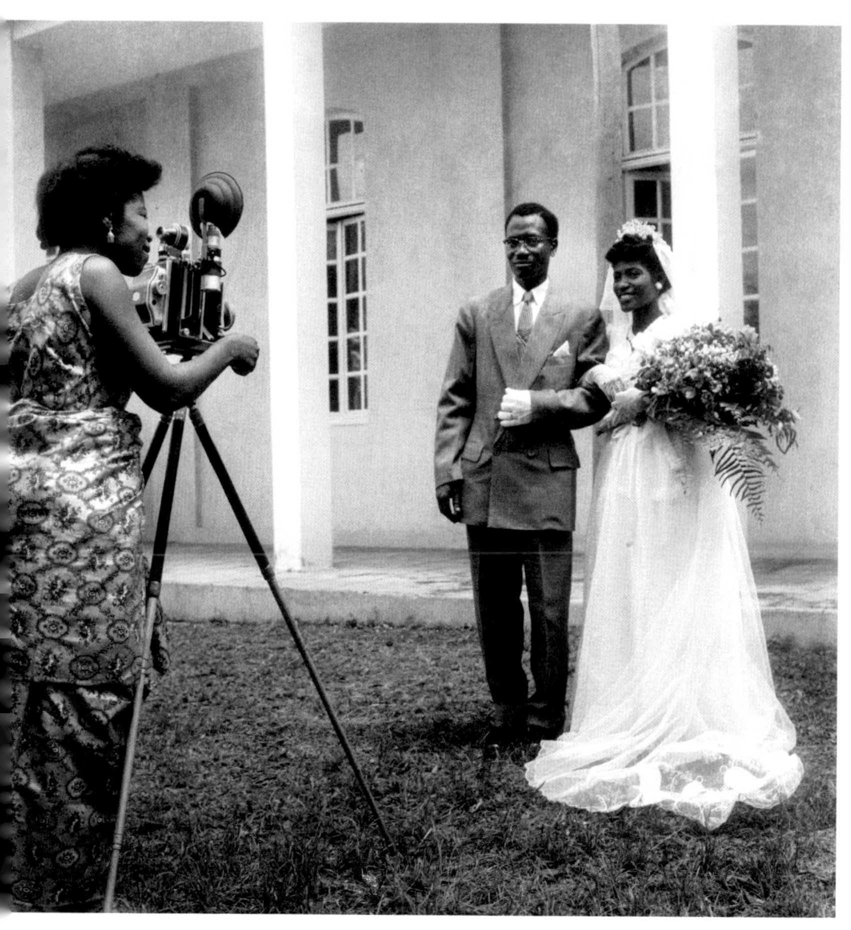

14. Jim Bailey and friends at a *Drum* party,
Chorkor beach, Accra, c. 1954–56.

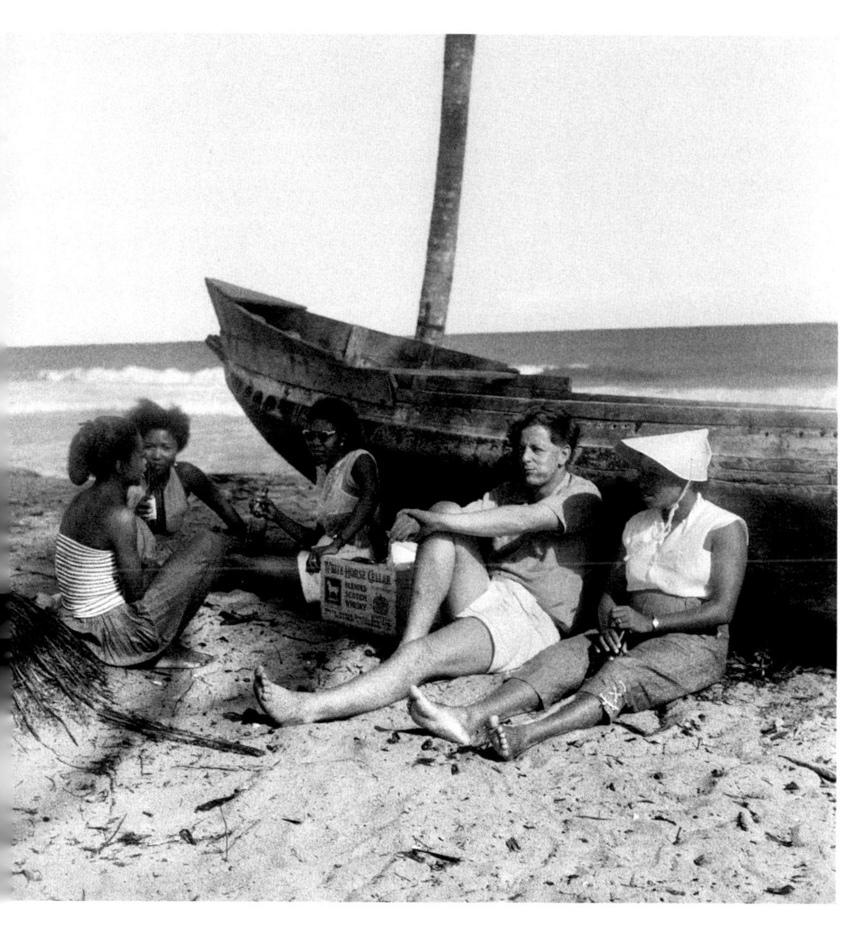
WHITE HORSE CELLAR
BLENDED
SCOTCH
WHISKY

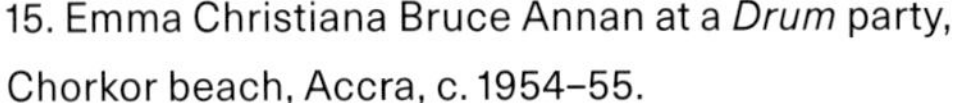

15. Emma Christiana Bruce Annan at a *Drum* party, Chorkor beach, Accra, c. 1954–55.

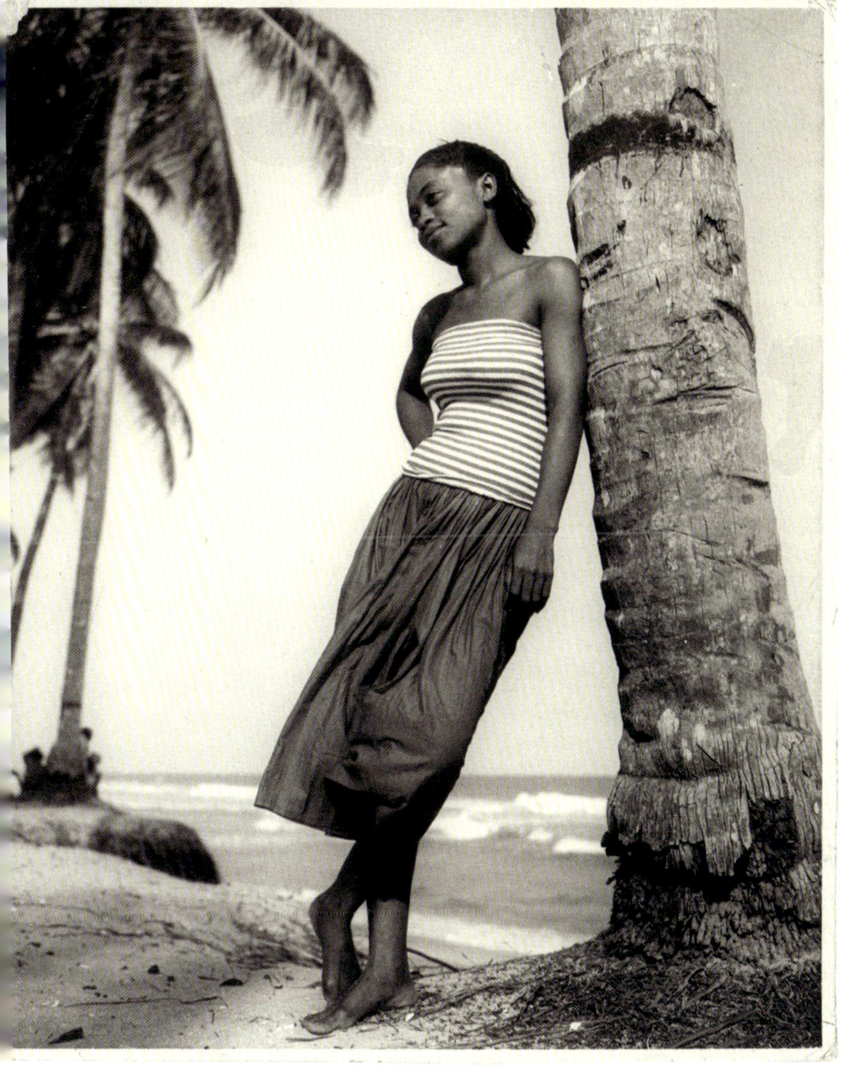

16. Self-portrait with a store assistant at the West African
Drug Company, central Accra, c. 1952.

Overleaf:
17. Kwame Nkrumah on his release from prison, with
members of the Convention People's Party (CPP), following
his victory in the Gold Coast elections, Accra, 1951.

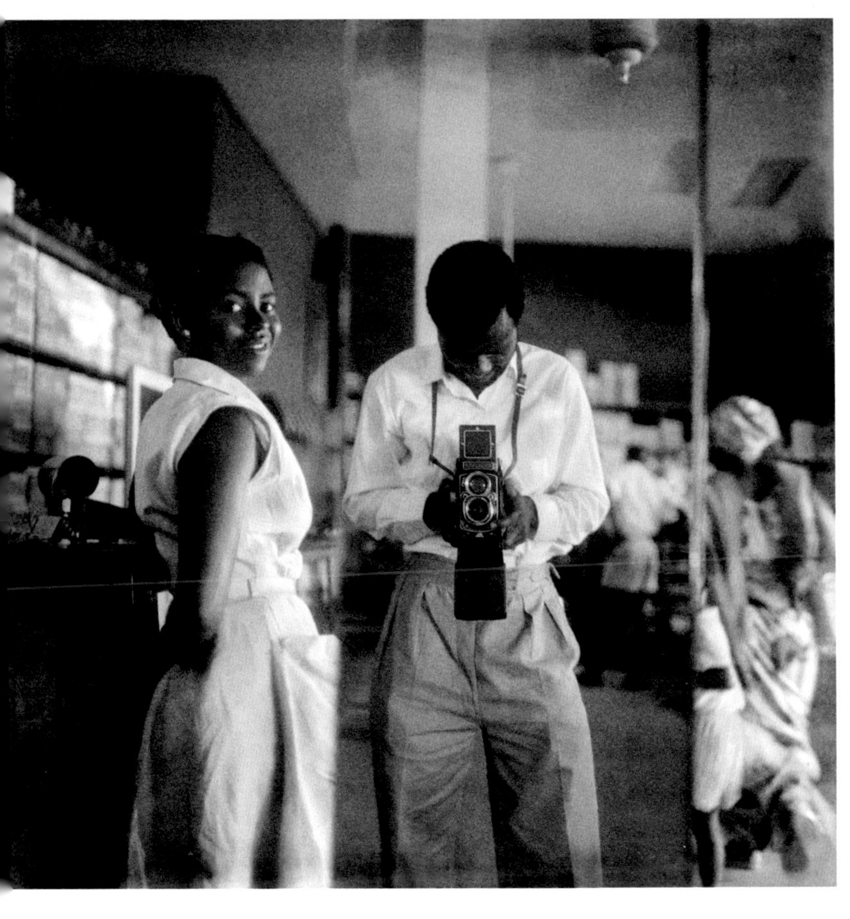

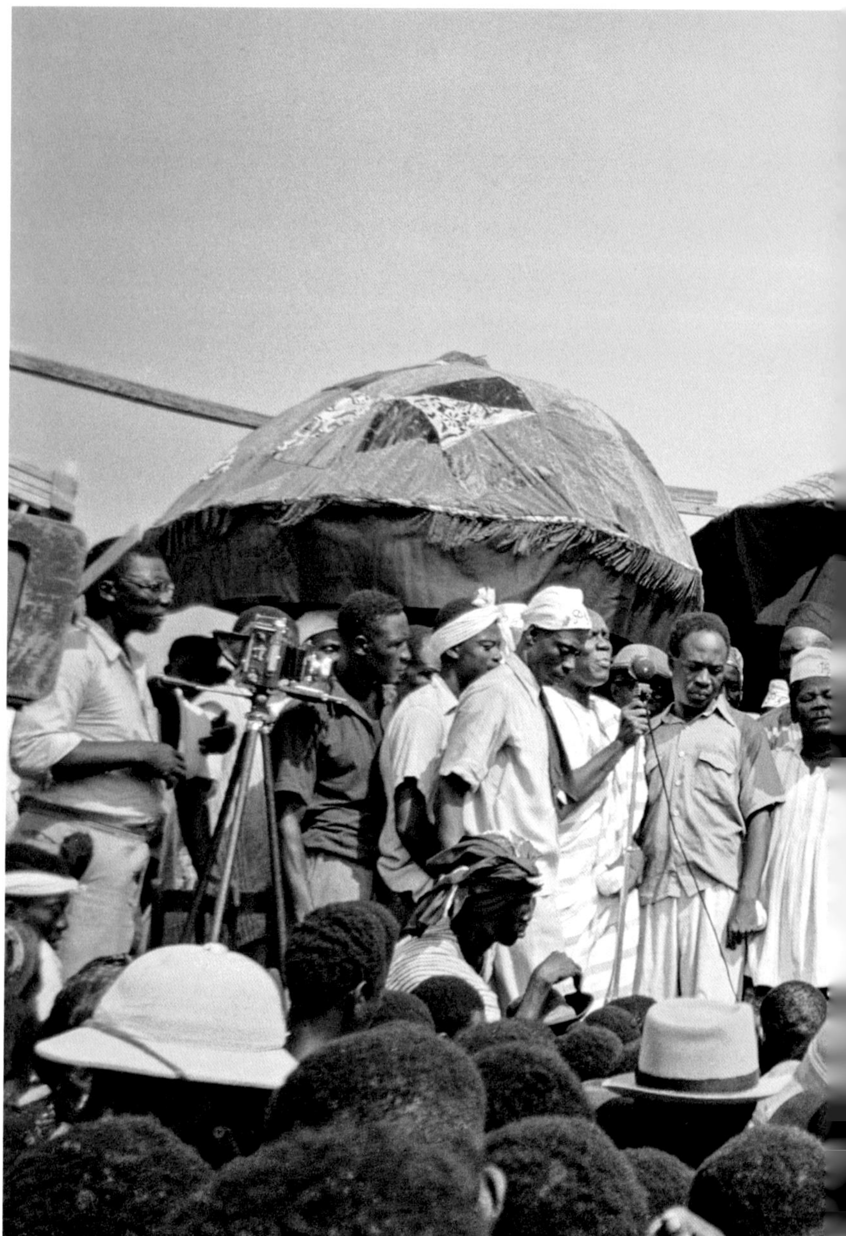

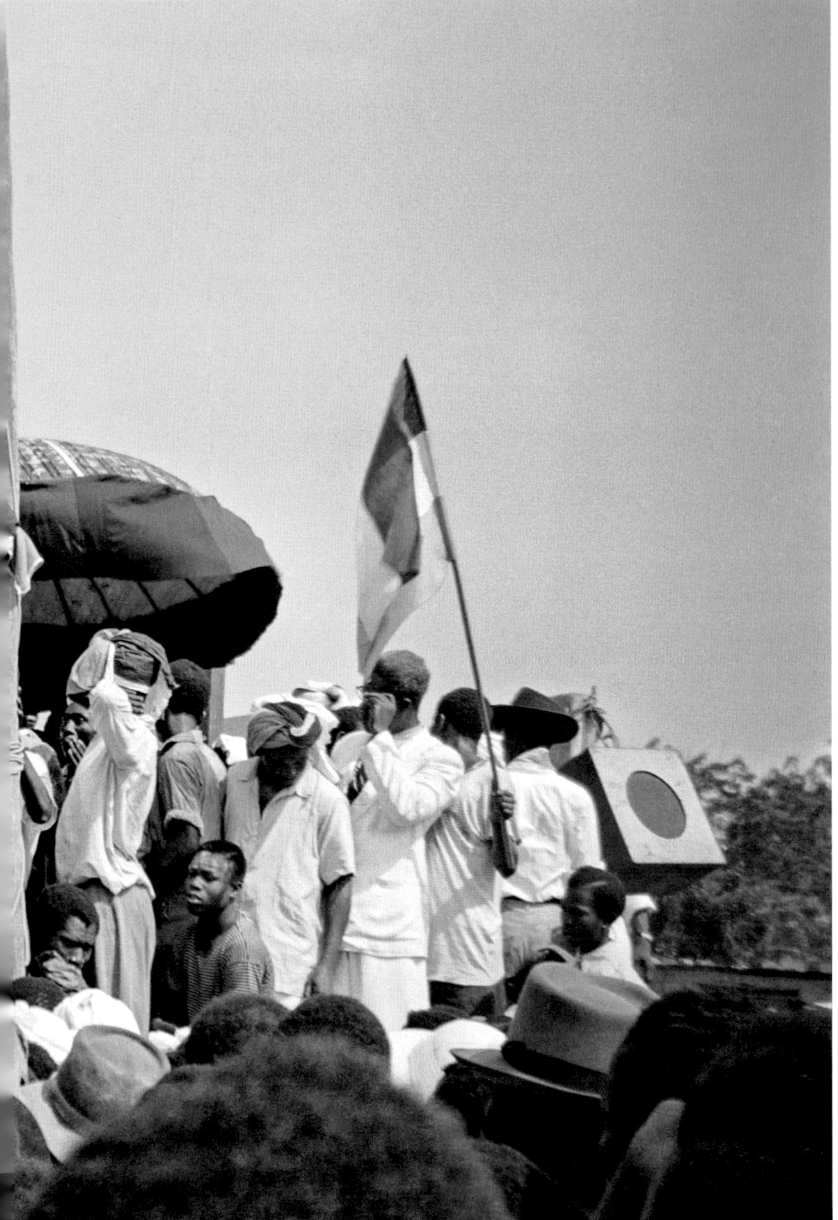

18. Oko Kolomashi posing with Kwame Nkrumah to express support
for the Convention People's Party at the parliamentary elections, 1954.

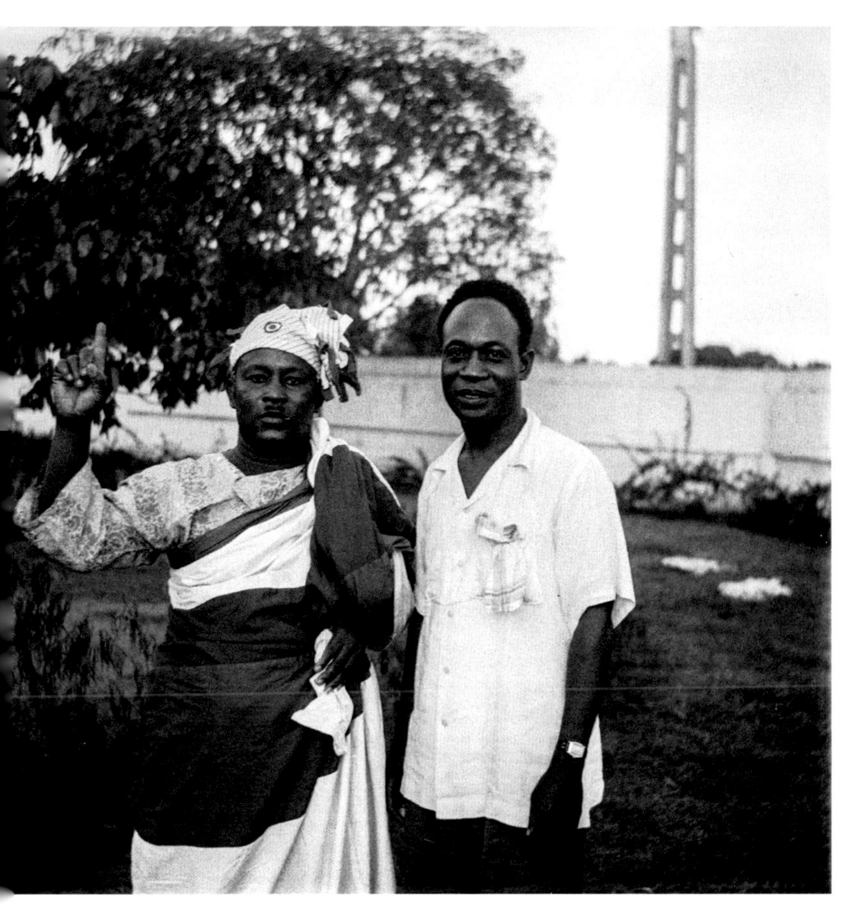

19. J.B. Danquah (left) and Obetsebi Lamptey (centre), members of
the 'Big Six', with Lamptey's daughter and secretary, Kyebi, 1950s.

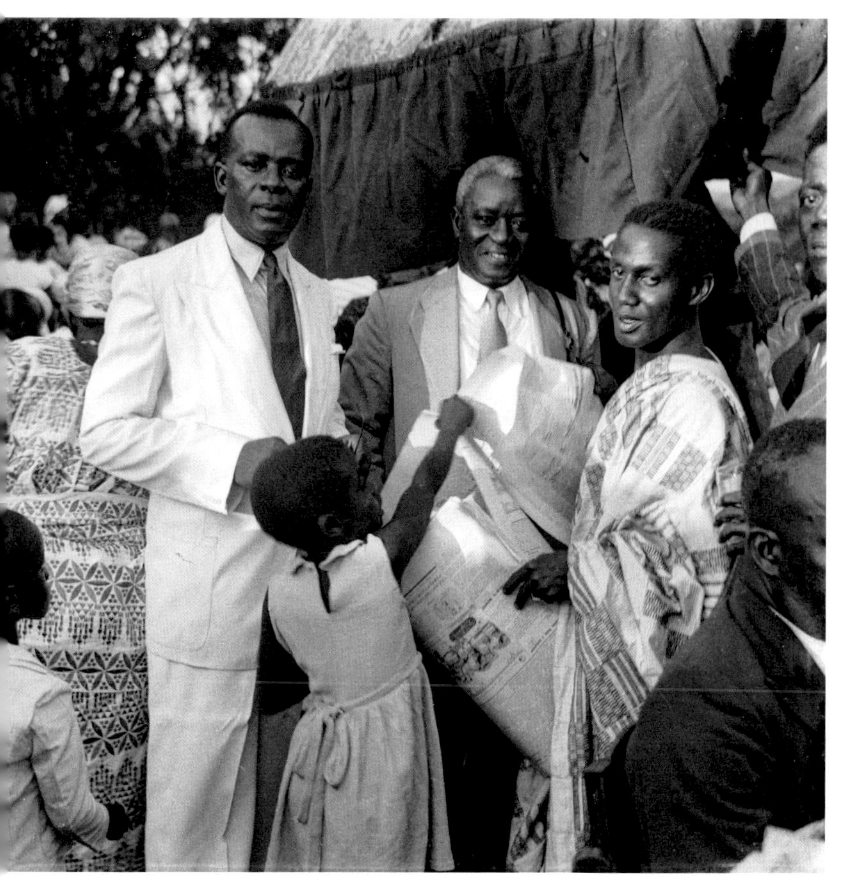

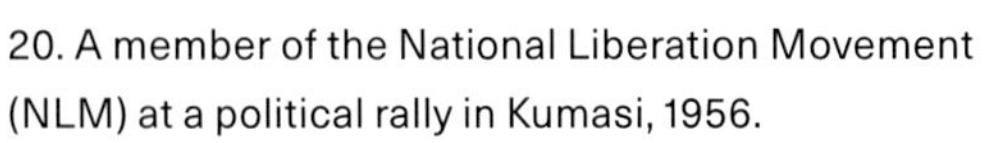

20. A member of the National Liberation Movement (NLM) at a political rally in Kumasi, 1956.

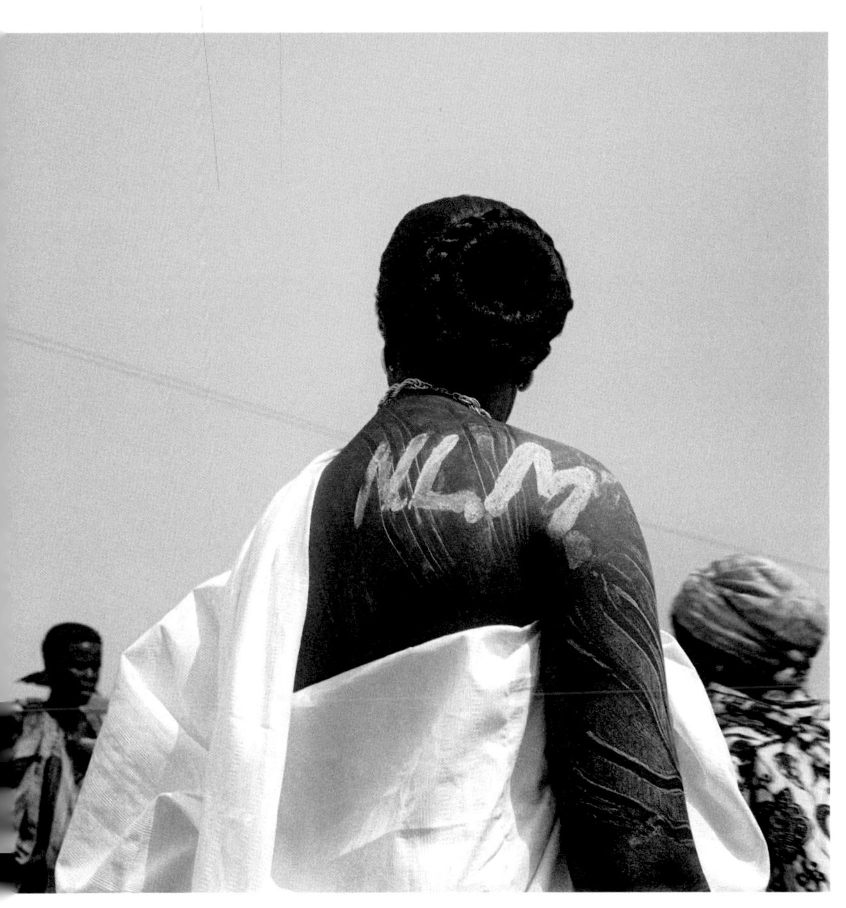
NLM

21. Kwame Nkrumah with the Duchess of Kent
and representatives of the British government at
independence celebrations in Accra, March 1957.

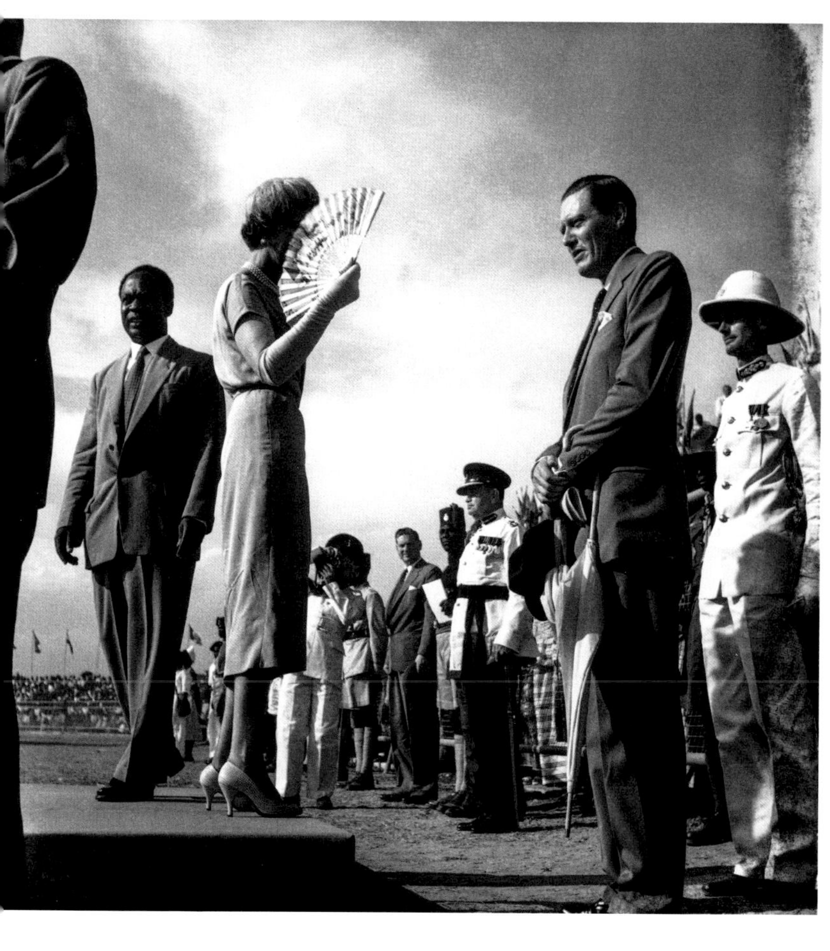

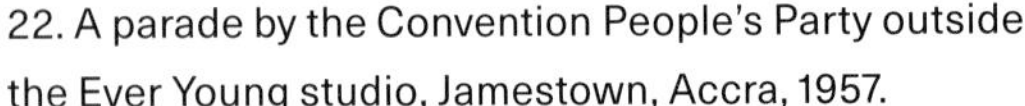

22. A parade by the Convention People's Party outside
the Ever Young studio, Jamestown, Accra, 1957.

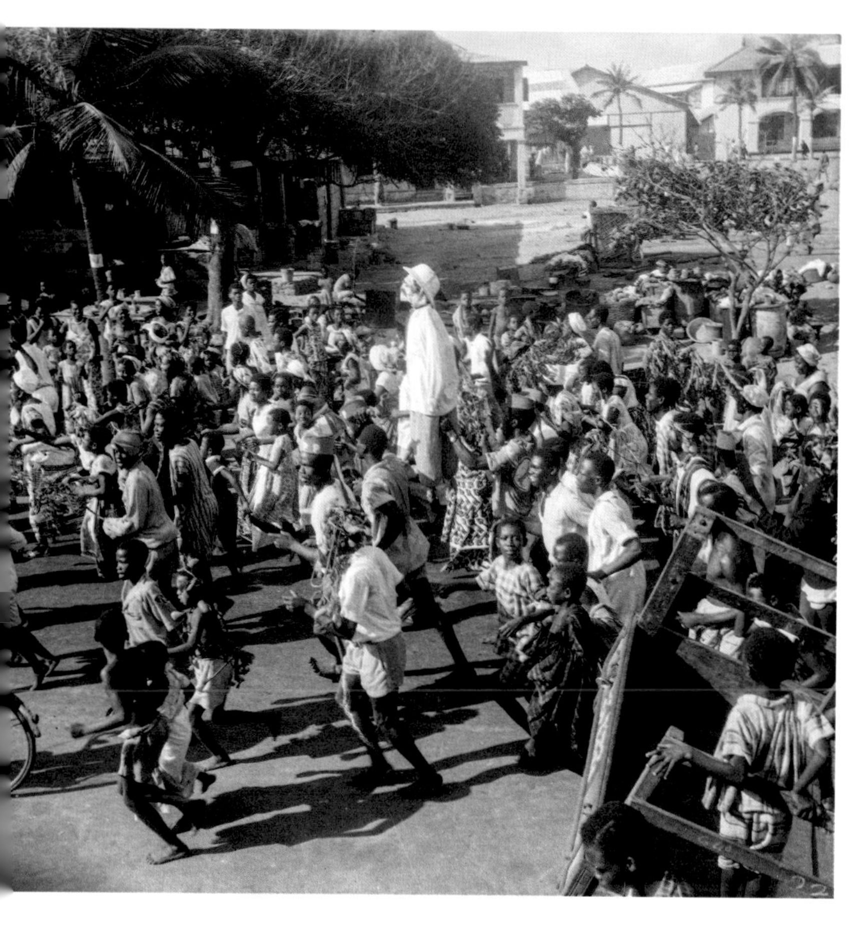

23. Self-portrait with Kwame Nkrumah, Roy Ankrah
and his wife Rebecca, Accra, c. 1952.

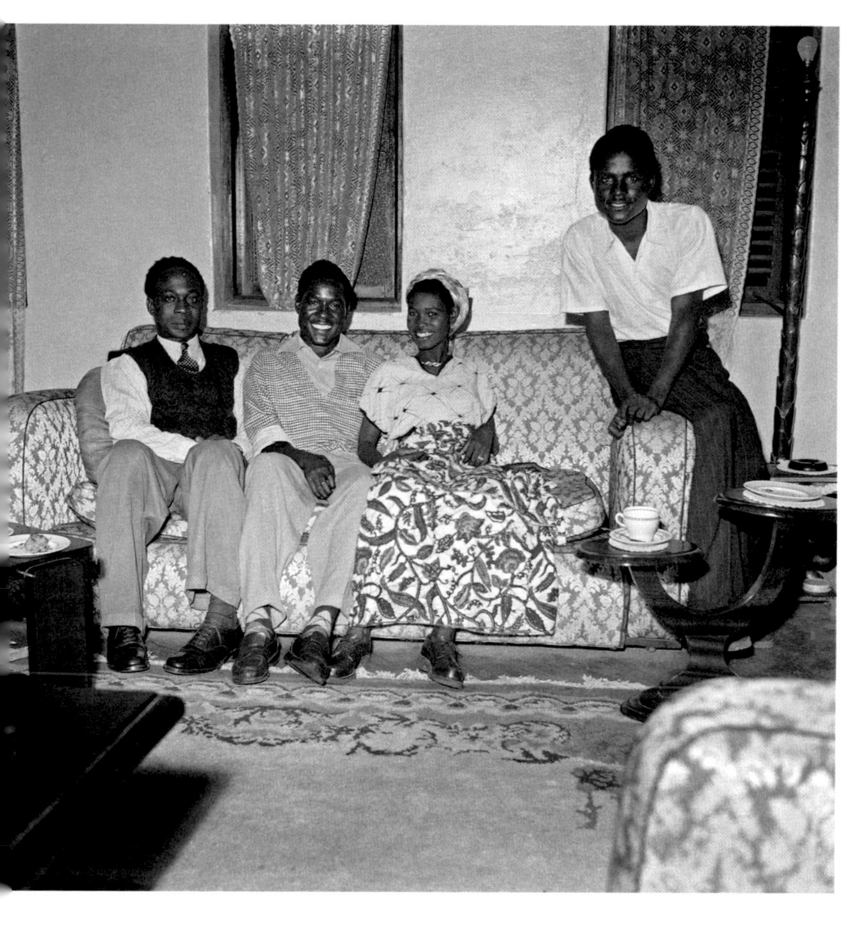

24. An African American tourist photographing the
Black Star Gate in Accra before the five-pointed
star was placed on top, c. 1958–59.

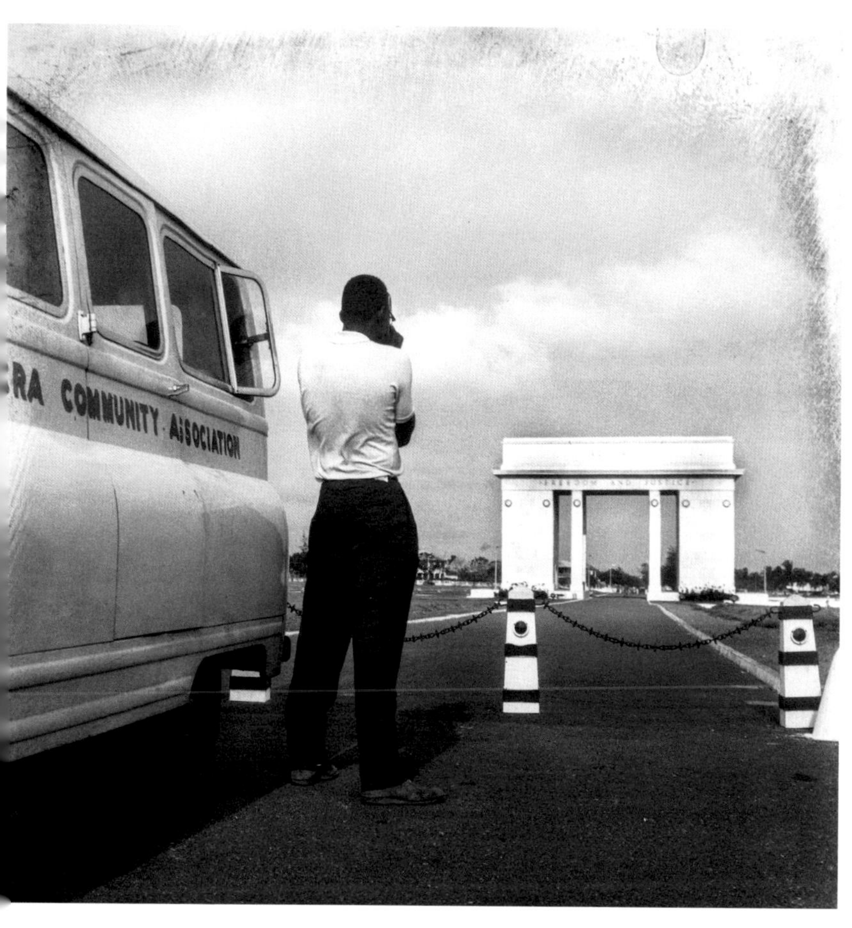
RA · COMMUNITY · ASSOCIATION
FREEDOM AND JUSTICE

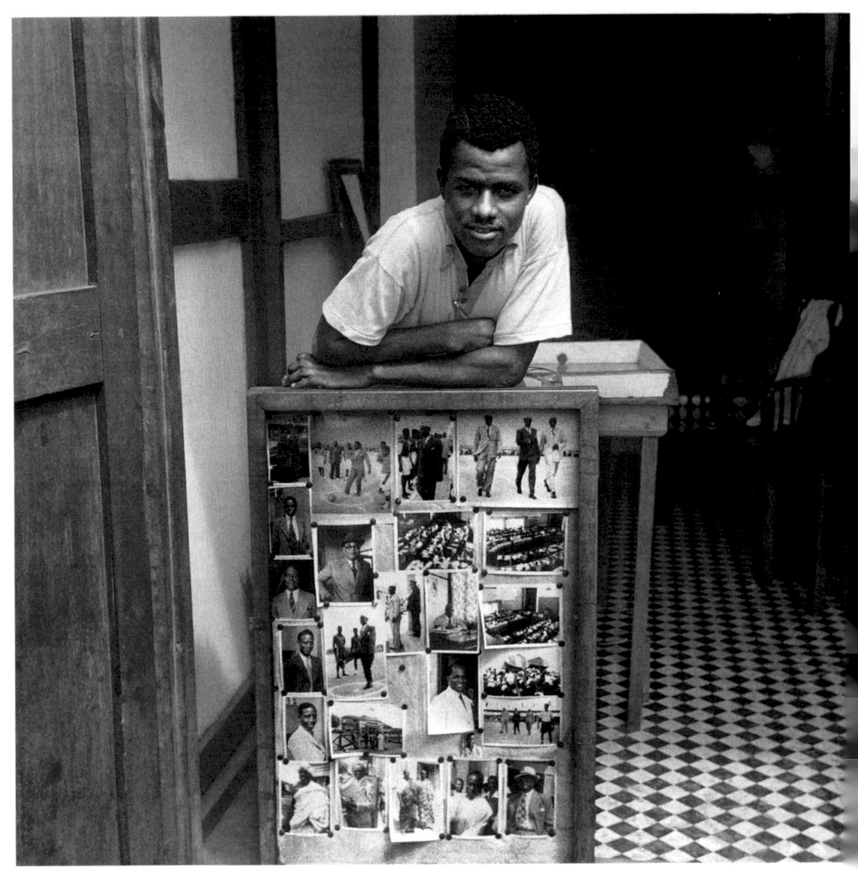

25. Portrait of James Barnor with a display board
borrowed from a Nigerian photographer friend,
Francis Eme, Jamestown, Accra, c. 1952.

26. Evelyn Abbew washing prints at the Ever Young
studio, Jamestown, Accra, c. 1954–56.

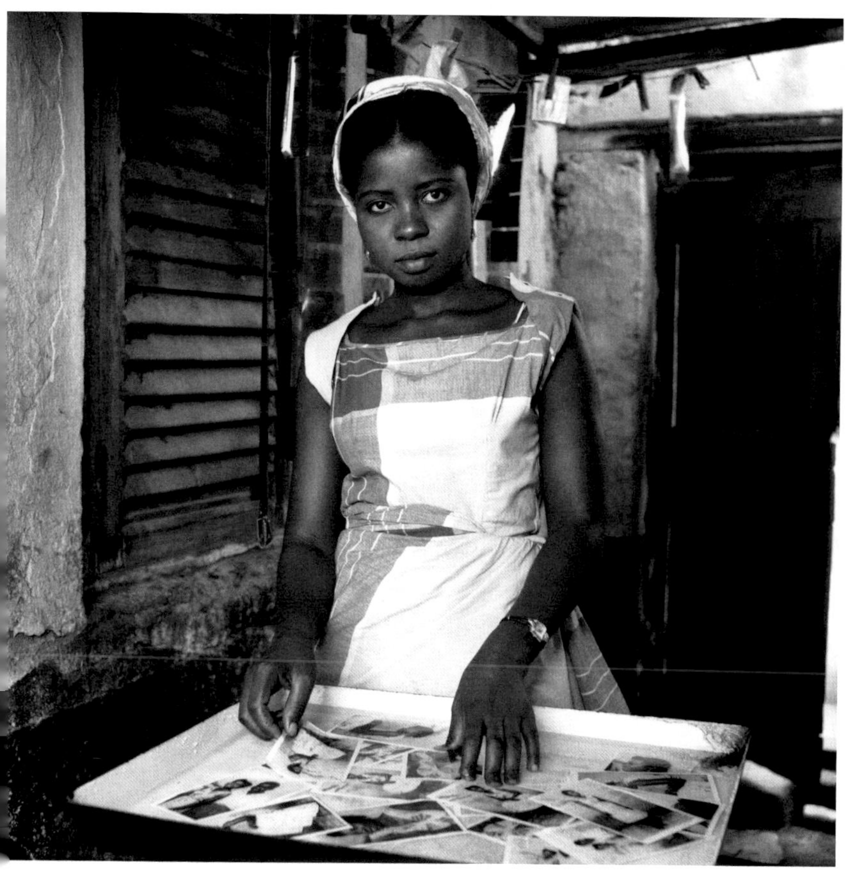

27. Self-portrait with a model during a training course
at the Agfa-Gevaert lab, Mortsel, Belgium, 1969.

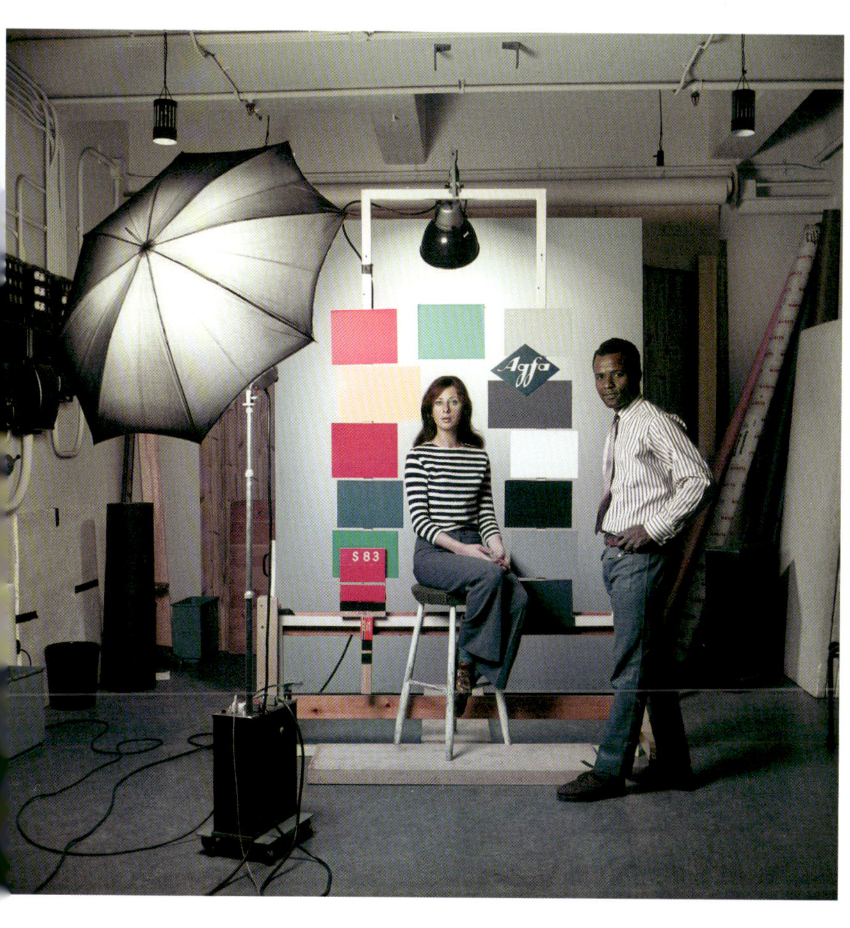

Agfa
S 83

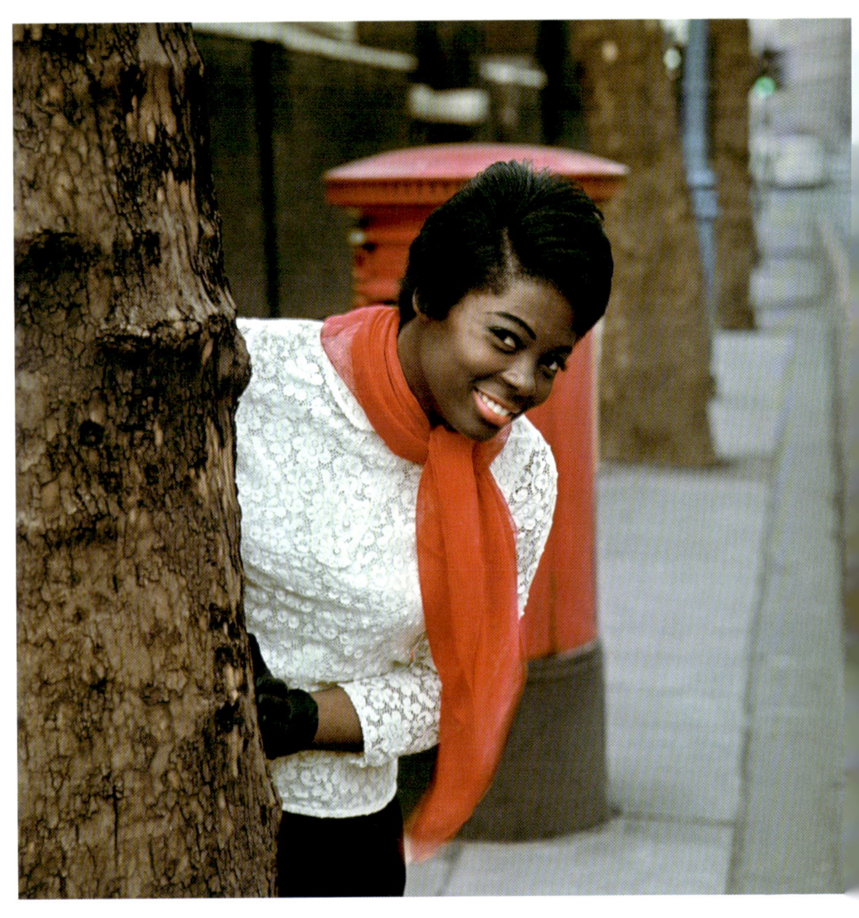

28. Rosemarie 'Funflower' Thompson,
Drum cover model, London, 1966.

29. Photo shoot with Erlin Ibreck at the Campbell
Drayton studio, Gray's Inn Road, London, 1967.

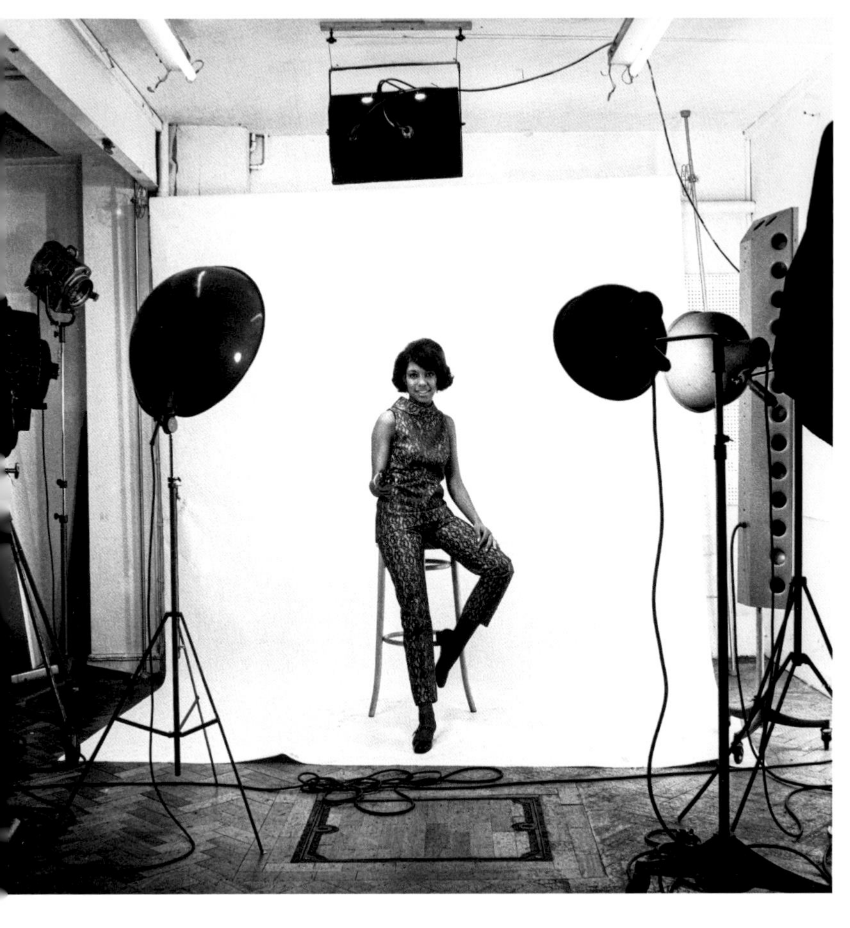

30. A group of friends after the wedding of
Mr and Mrs Sackey, Balham, London, 1966.

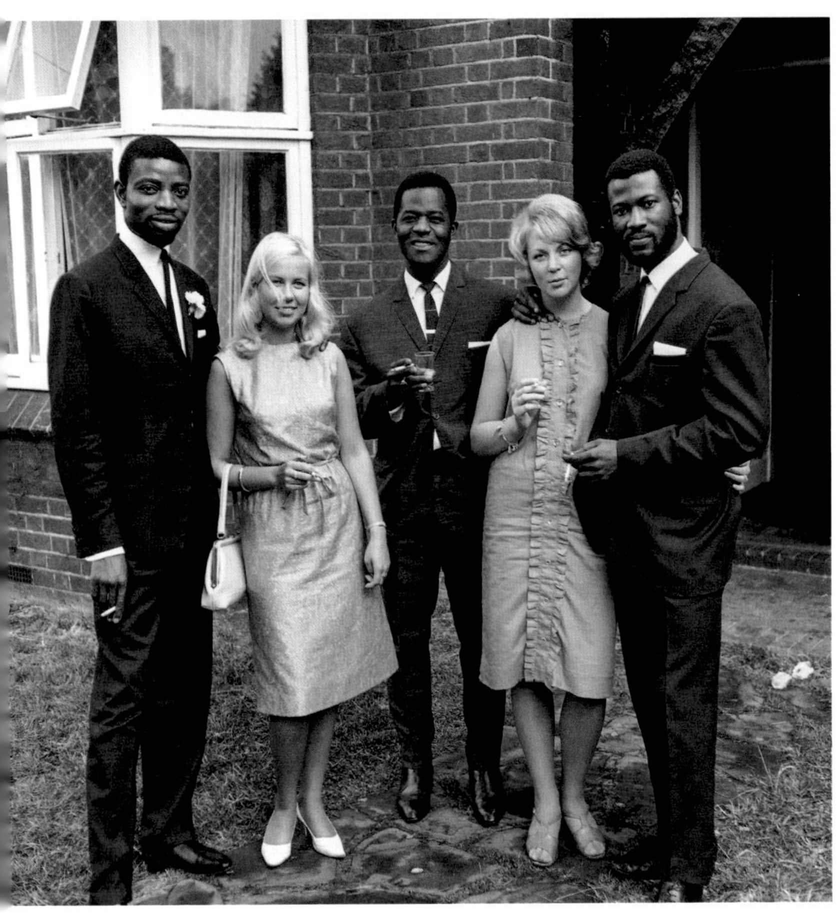

31. At a country fair in Wales, c. 1962.

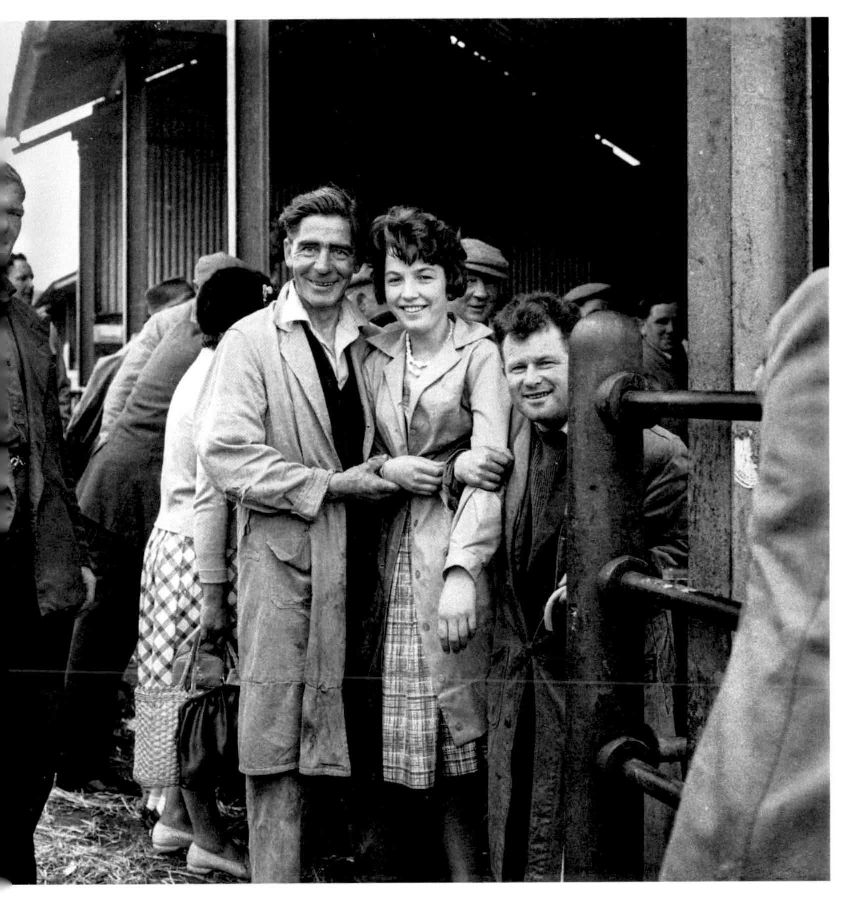

32. Rema Nelson, *Drum* cover model, at a
test shoot in Battersea Park, London, 1966.

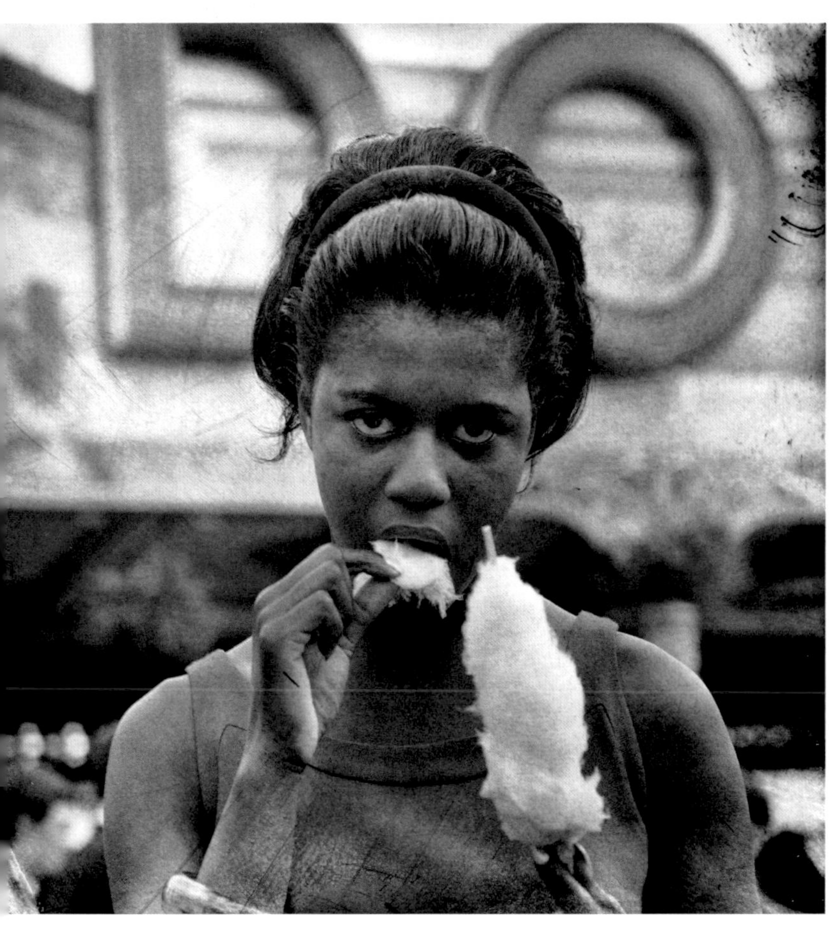

33. Eva, London, 1960s.

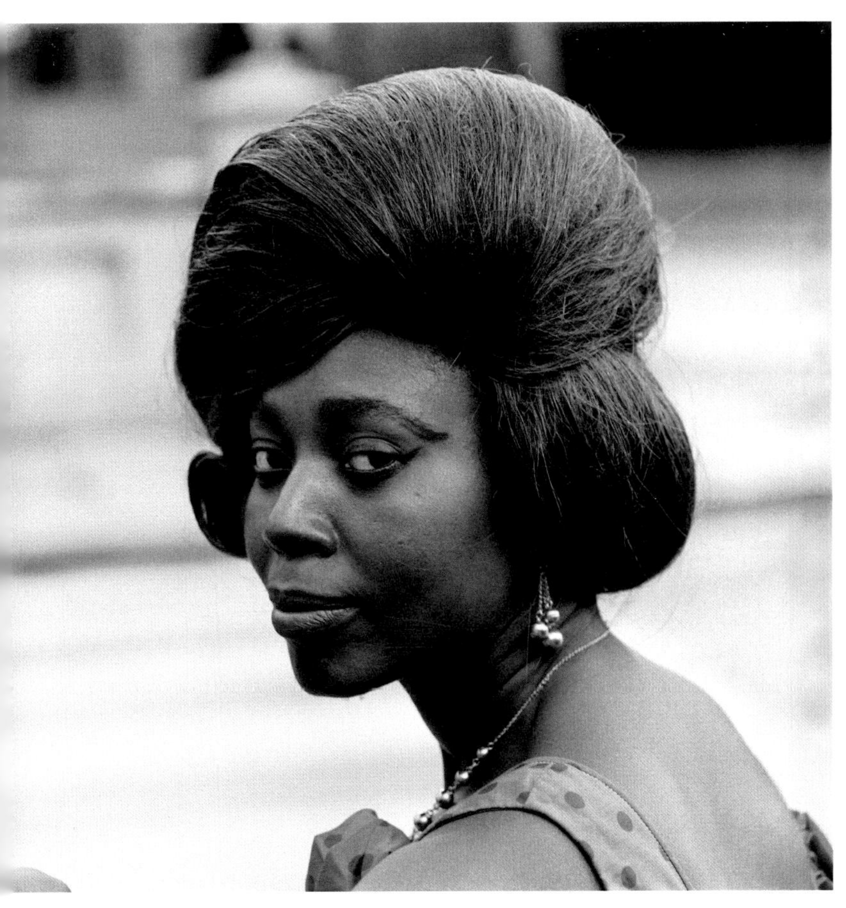

34. A Nigerian friend models for James Barnor at
Medway College of Art, Rochester, c. 1964–65.

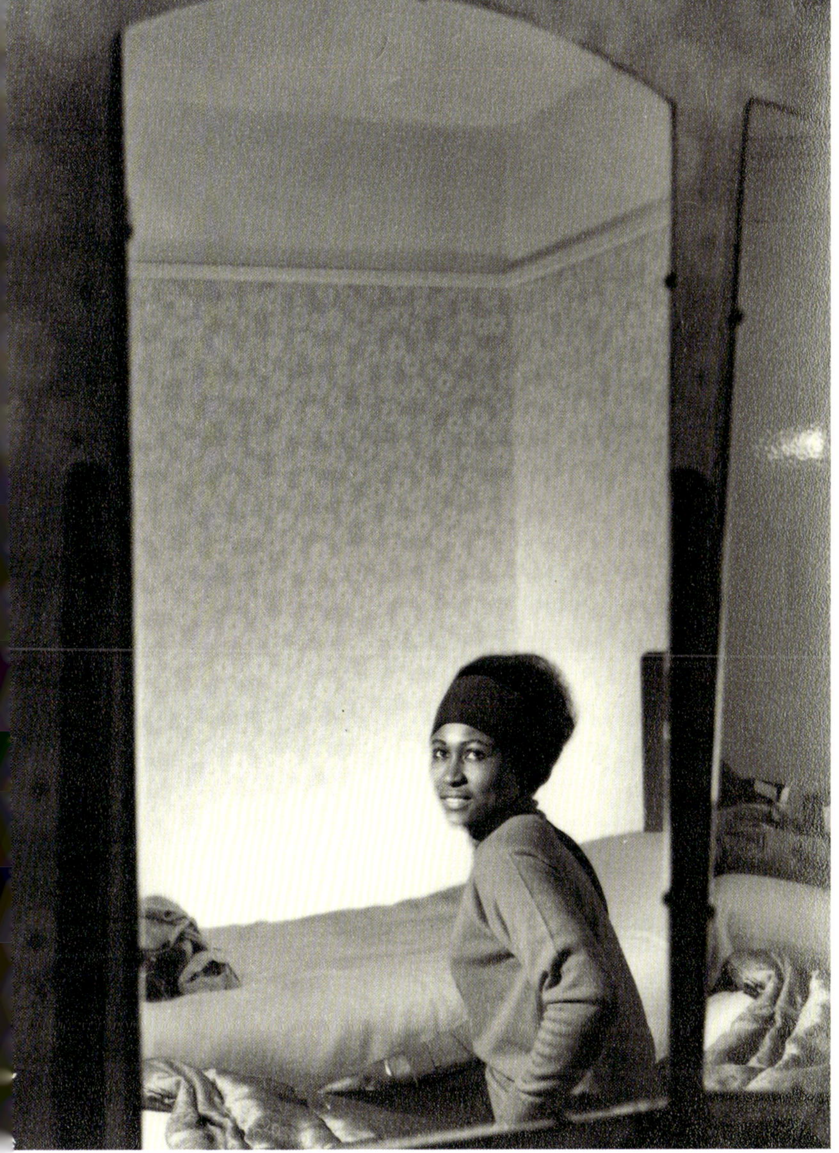

35. Untitled, London, 1960s.

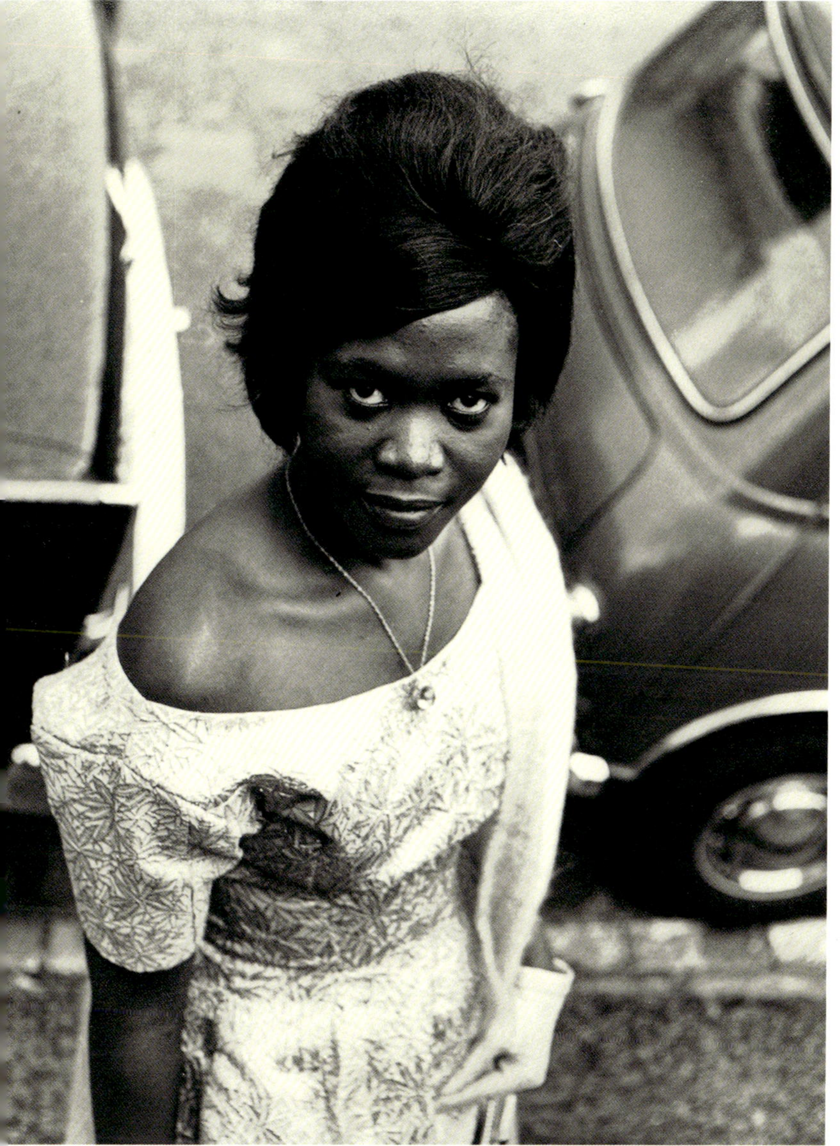

36. Double portrait of a Nigerian friend at
Medway College of Art, Rochester, c. 1963.

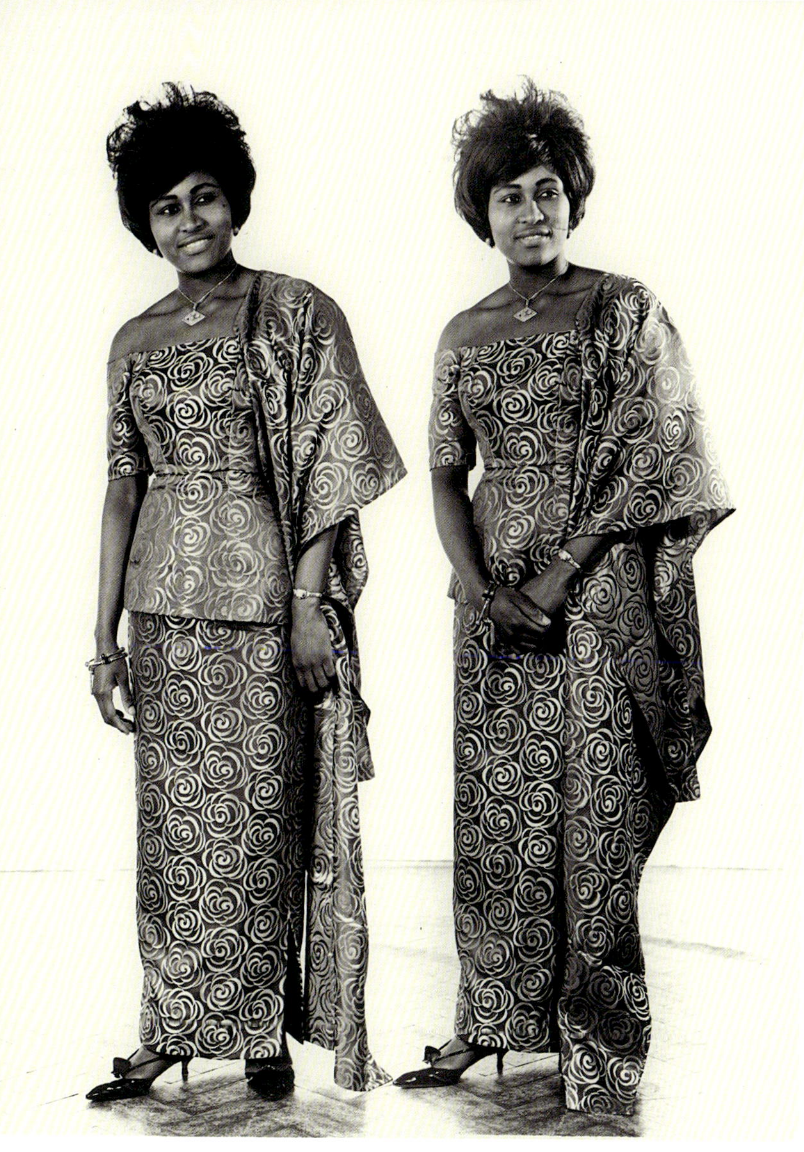

37. A model posing for *Drum* magazine,
Battersea Park, London, 1965.

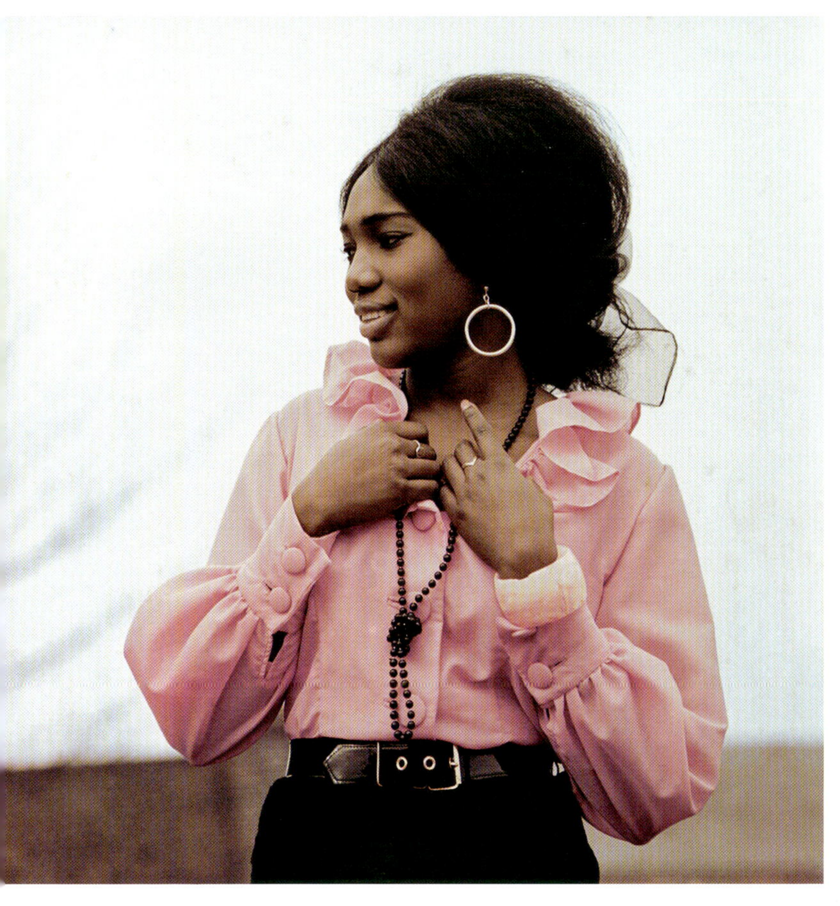

38. Three Indian gynaecologists at a
medical conference, London, 1960s.

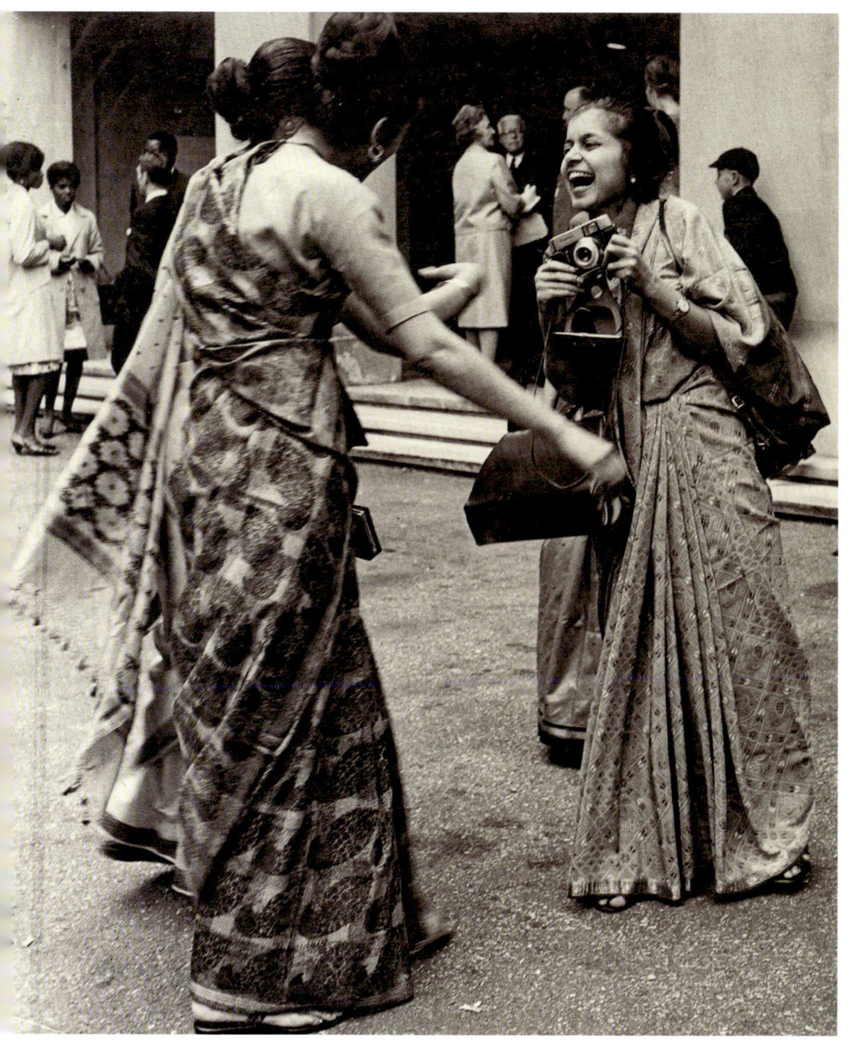

39. Portrait of Gladys Tshuba Brown,
Drum cover model, London, 1966.

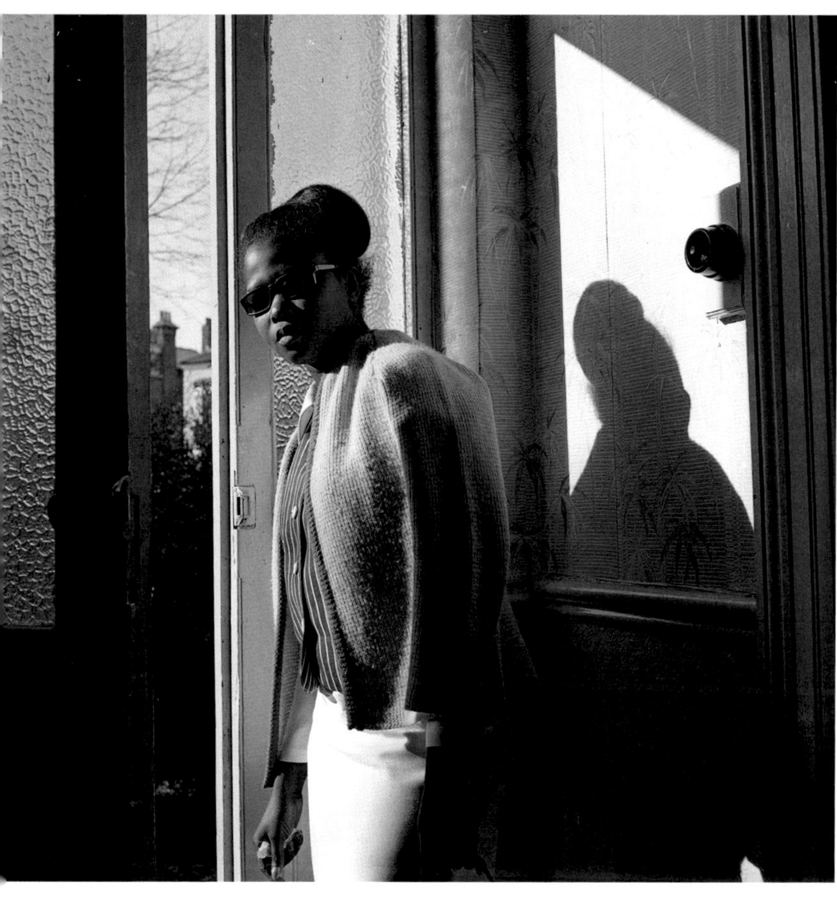

40. Muhammad Ali training for his fight against
Brian London at Earls Court, London, 1966.

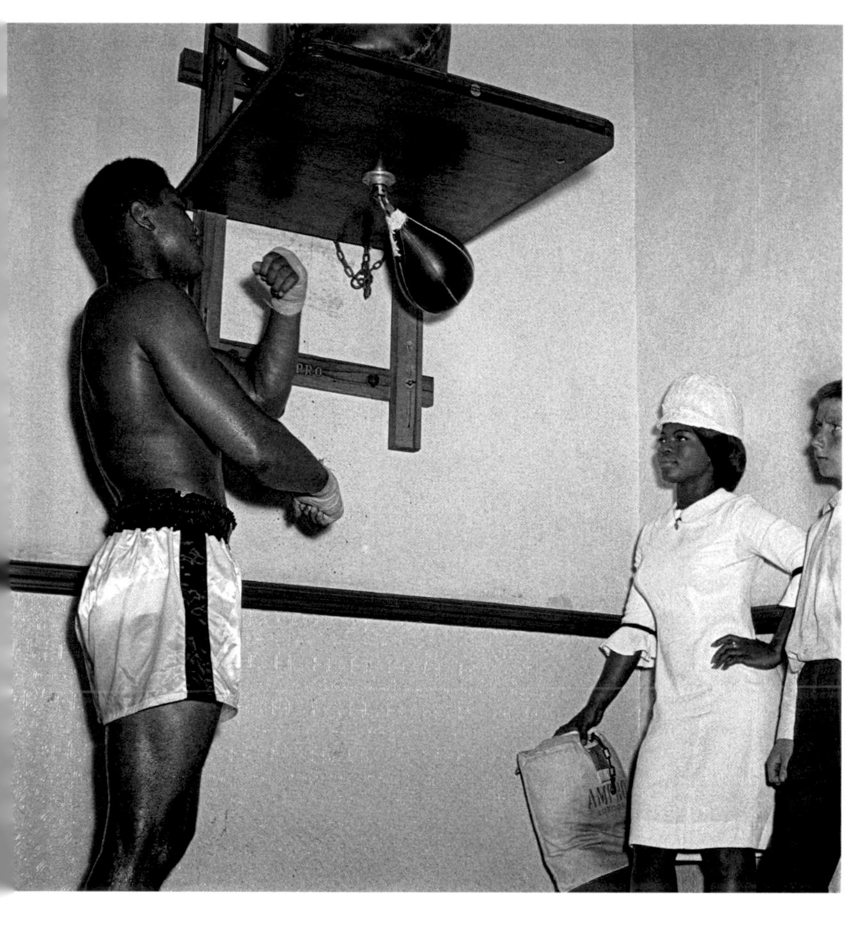

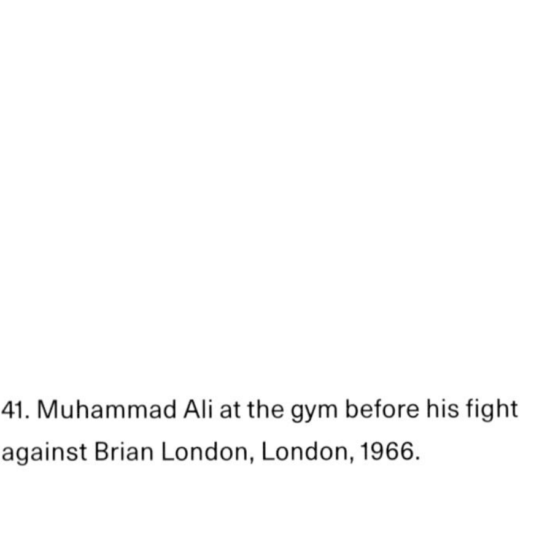

41. Muhammad Ali at the gym before his fight
against Brian London, London, 1966.

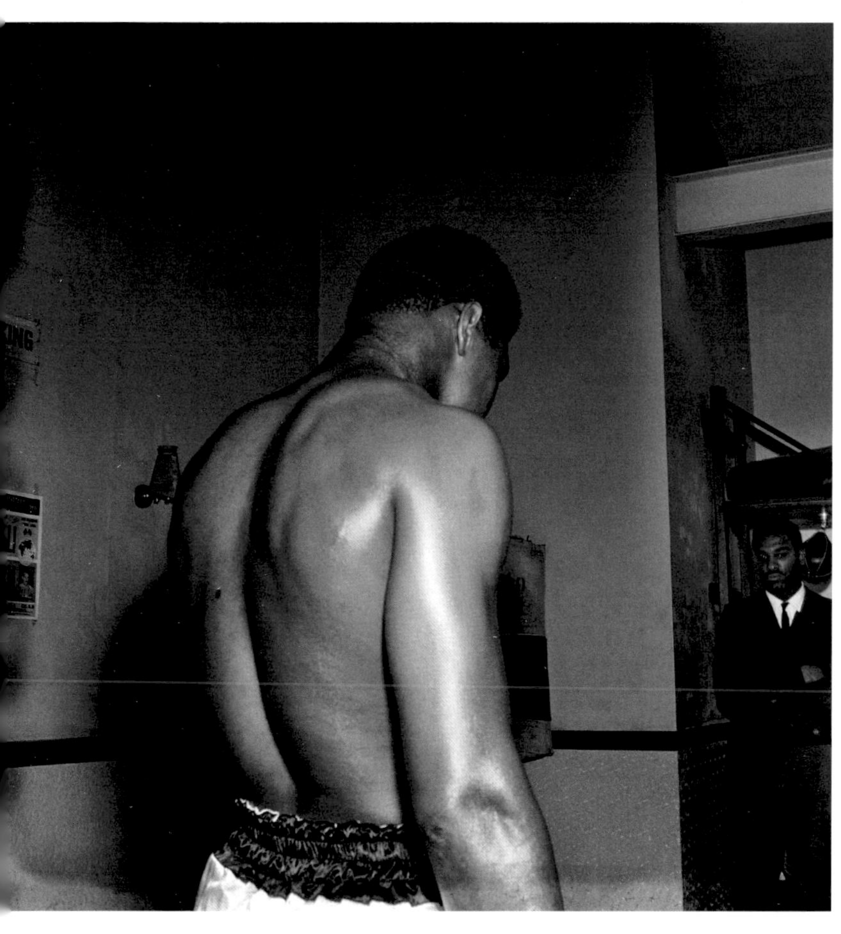

42. Erlin Ibreck, *Drum* cover model,
Kilburn, London, 1966.

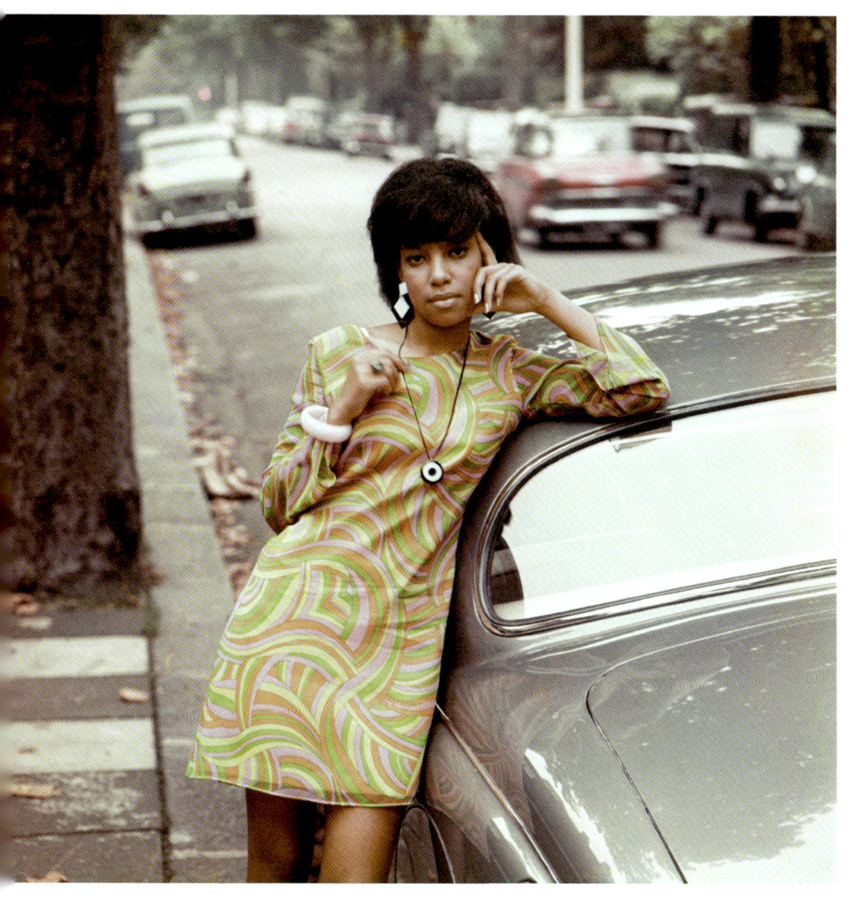

43. Constance Mulondo poses for *Drum*
after a concert by the Millionaires, London, 1967.

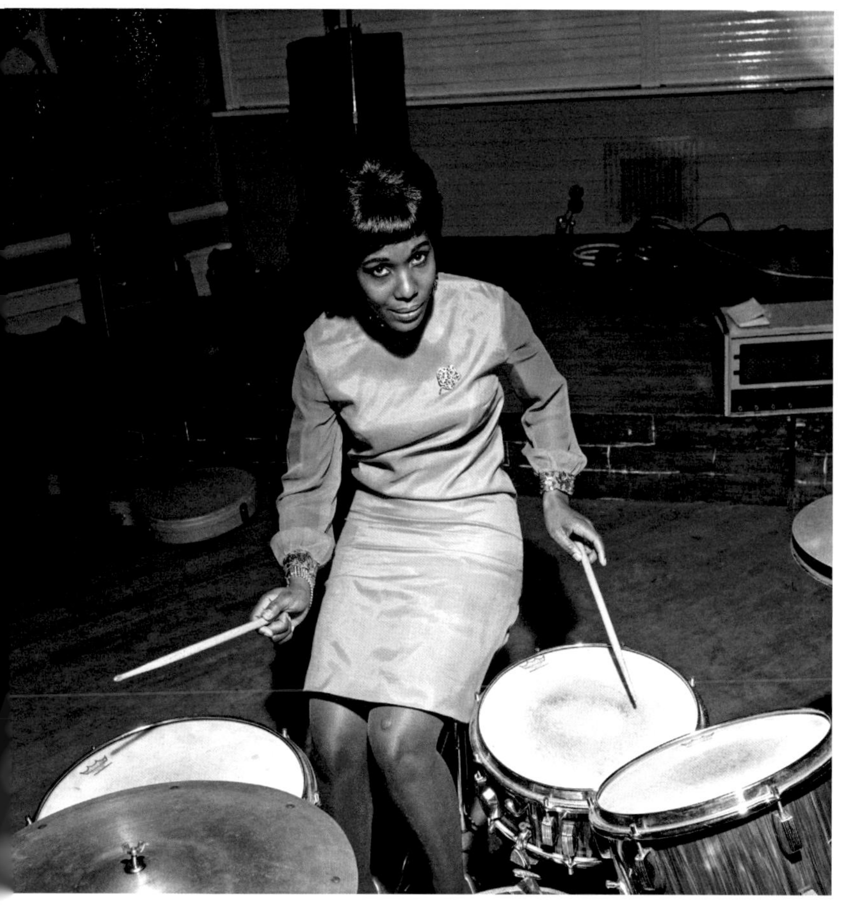

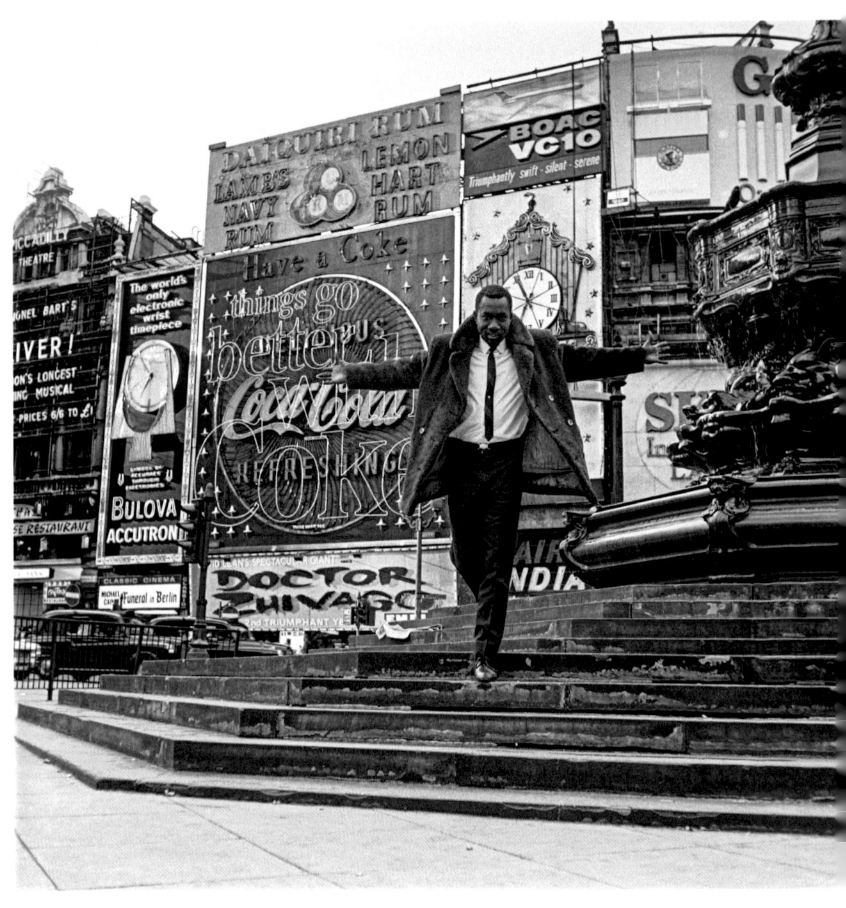

44. Mike Eghan photographed for *Drum*
at Piccadilly Circus, London, 1967.

45. Erlin Ibreck, *Drum* cover model,
at Petticoat Lane Market, London, 1966.

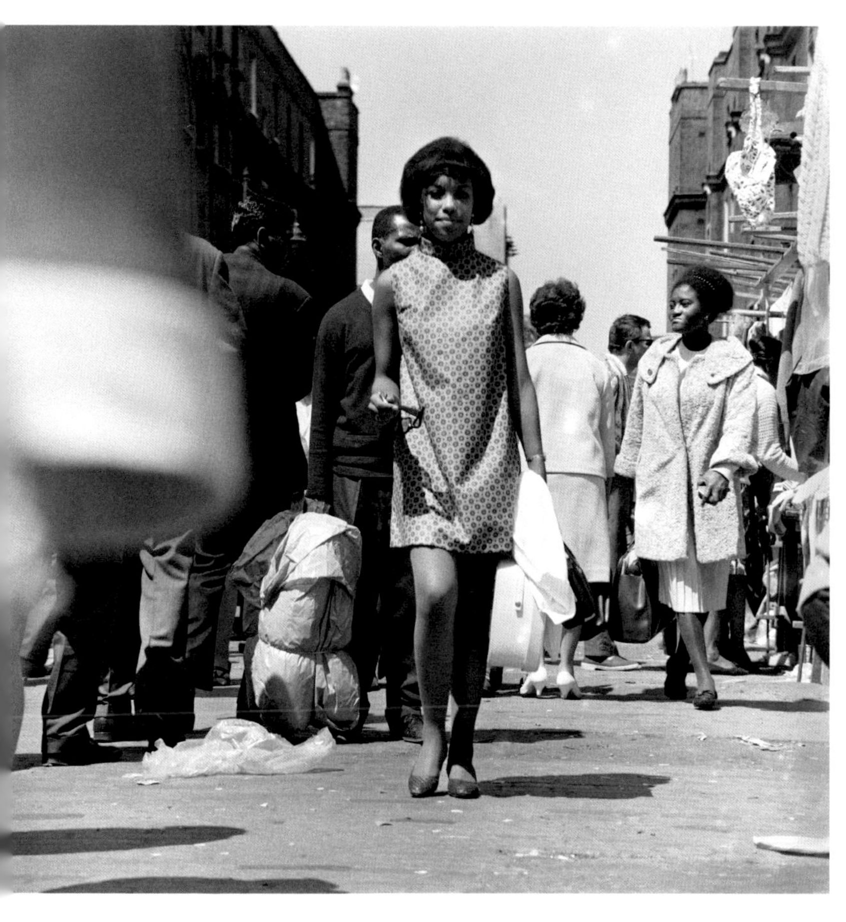

46. Portrait of James Barnor, UK, 1960s,
photographer unknown.

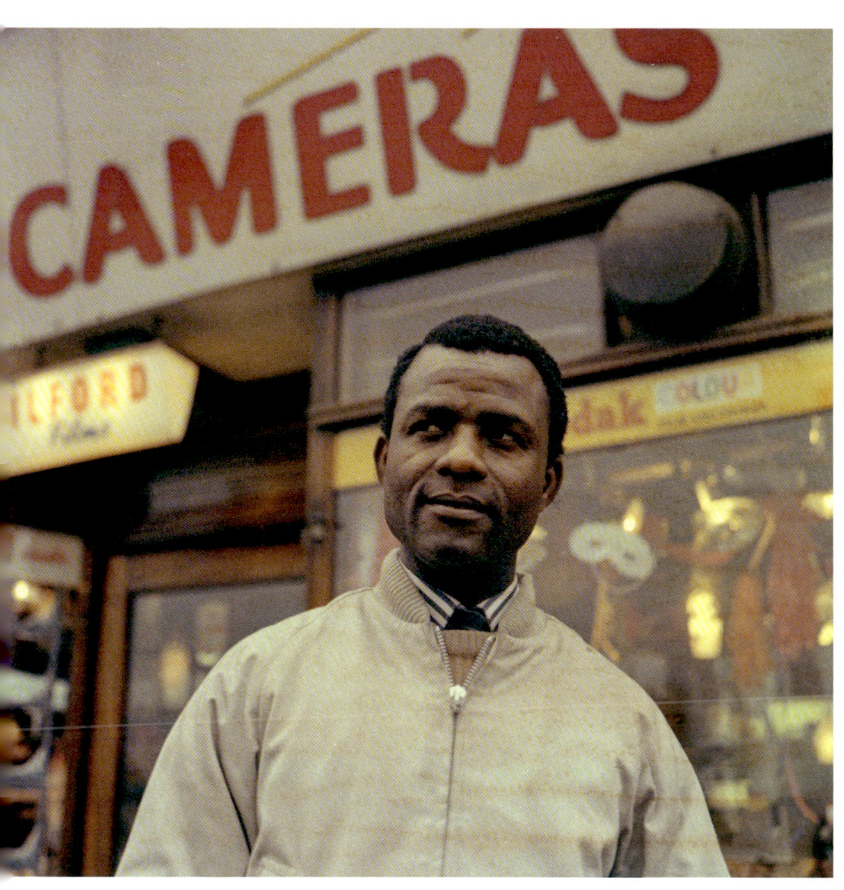

CAMERAS

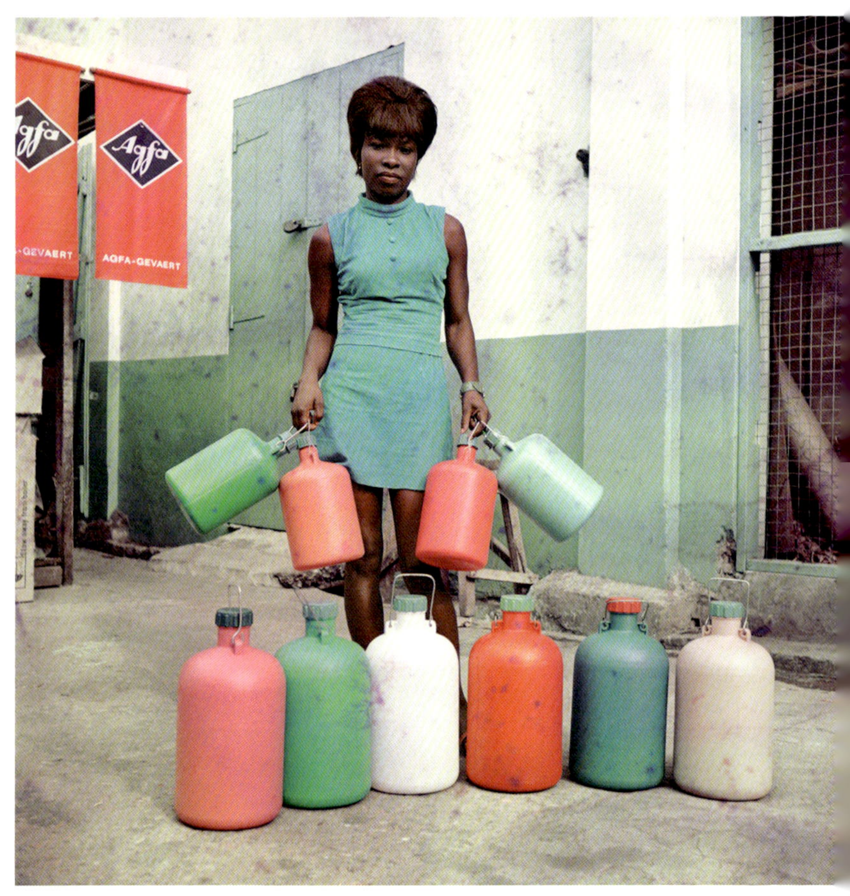

47. Sick-Hagemeyer shop assistant, Accra, c. 1970.

48. Mavis and Mary Barnor with an Agfa advertising
balloon, Accra, 1970.

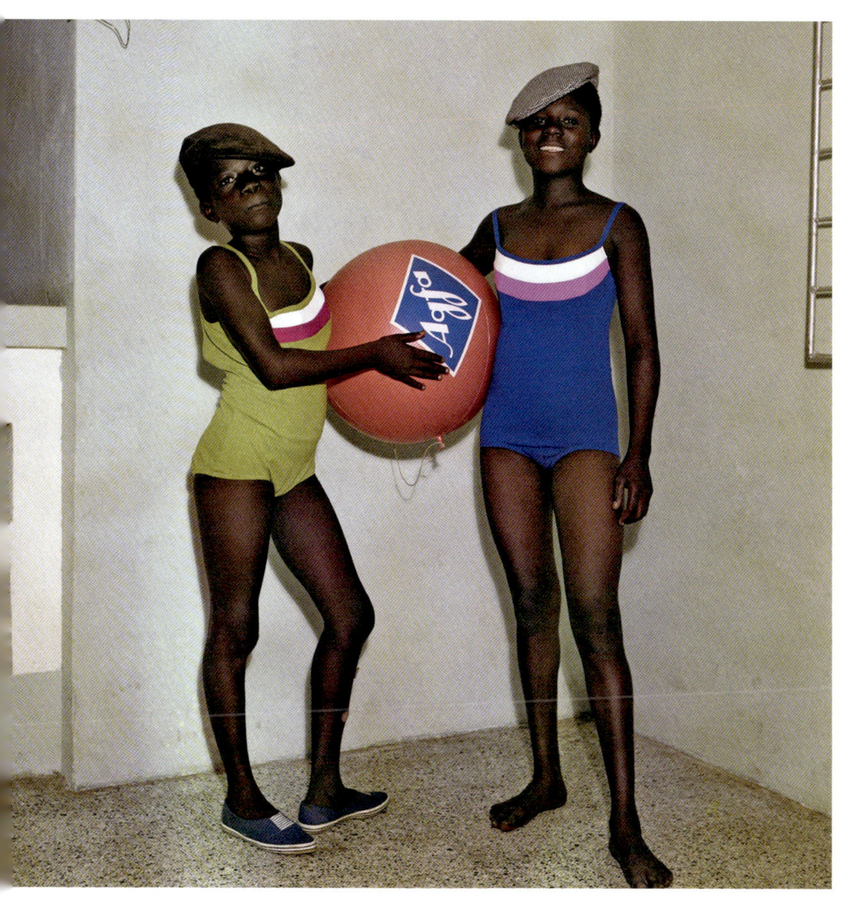

Agfa

49. At Ataa Quarcoopome's, Accra, 1974.

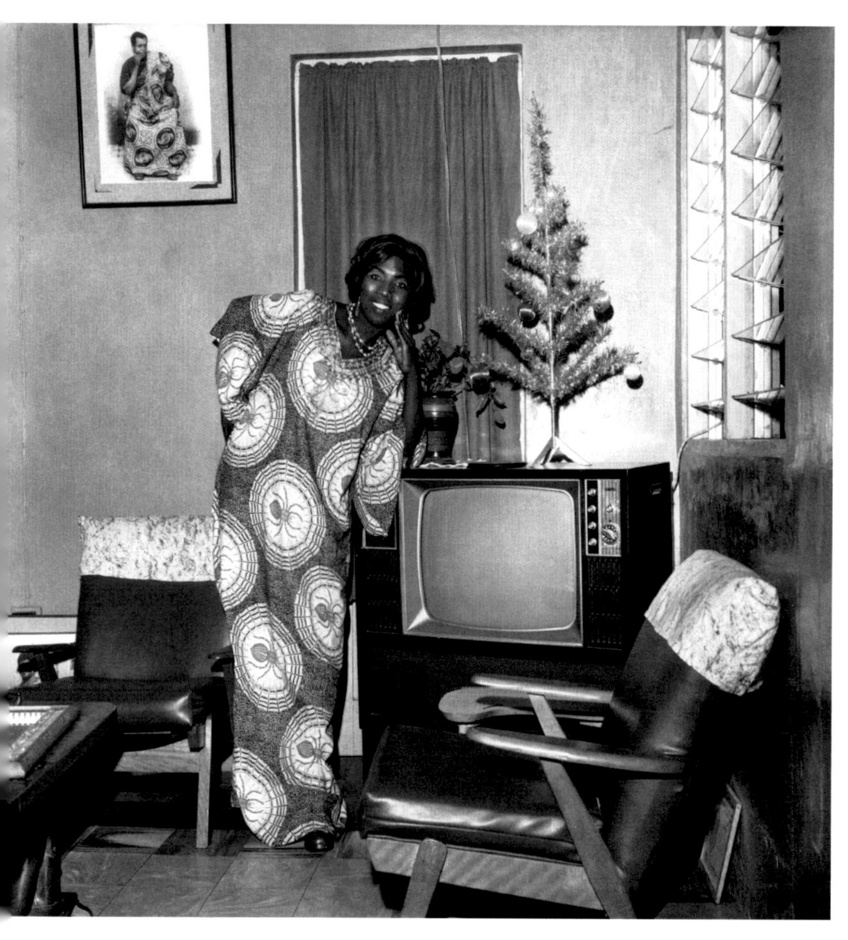

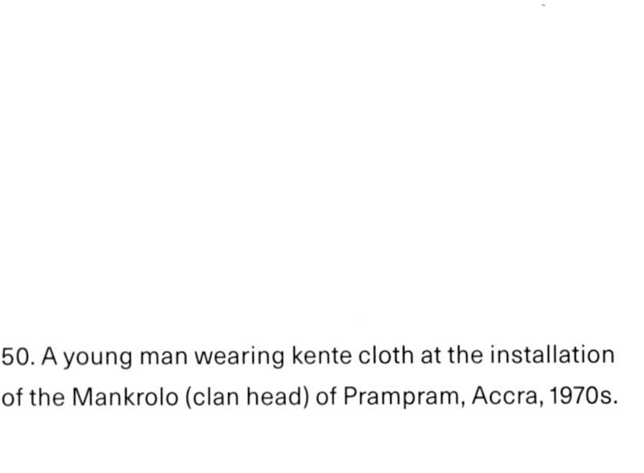

50. A young man wearing kente cloth at the installation
of the Mankrolo (clan head) of Prampram, Accra, 1970s.

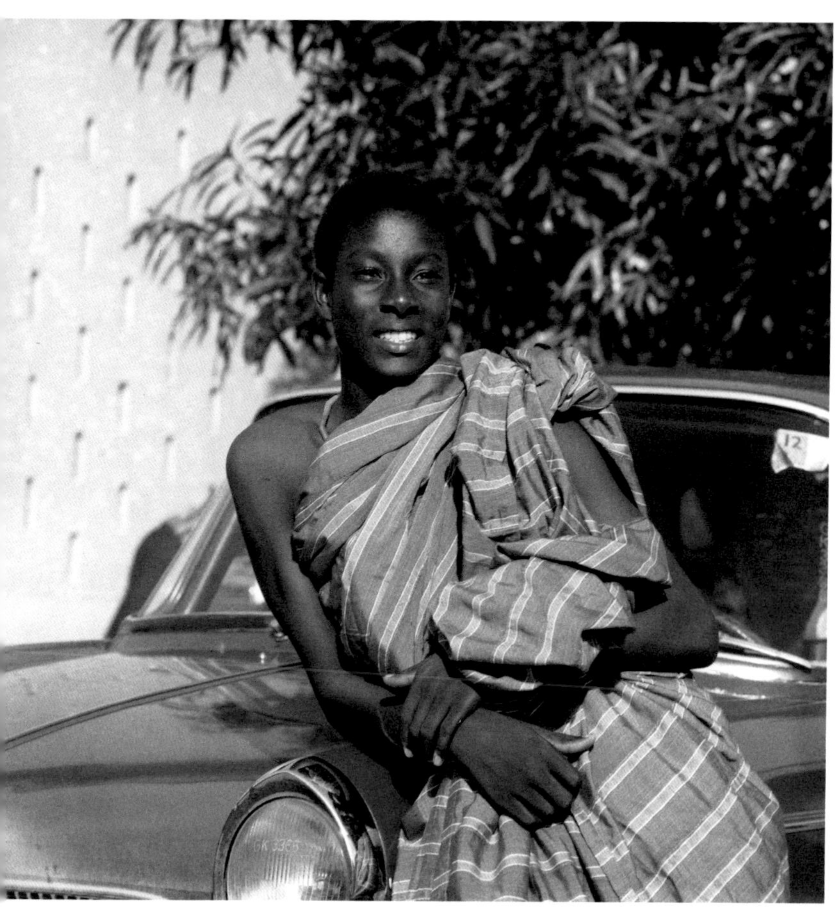

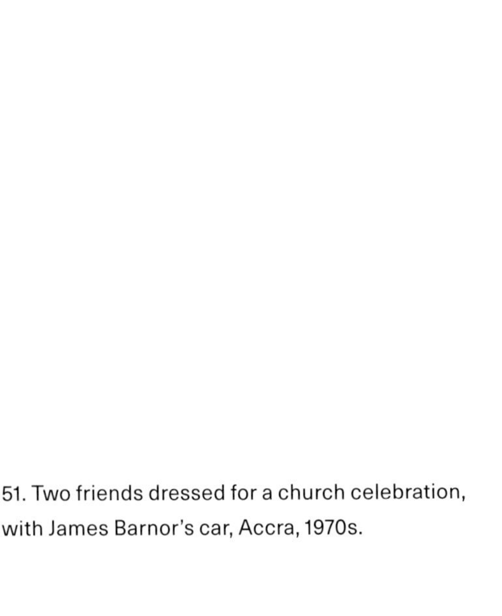

51. Two friends dressed for a church celebration,
with James Barnor's car, Accra, 1970s.

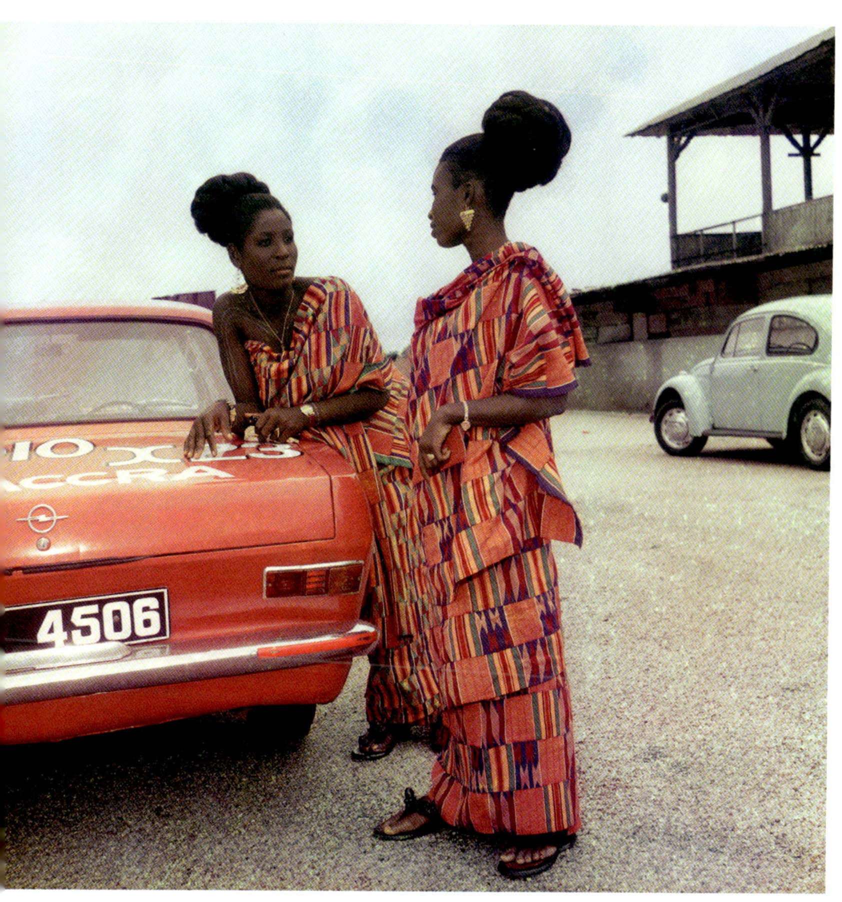

52. Pioneering Ghanaian photographer N.T. Clerk (right)
and friend, Asafoatse Nettey Road, Accra, c. 1974.

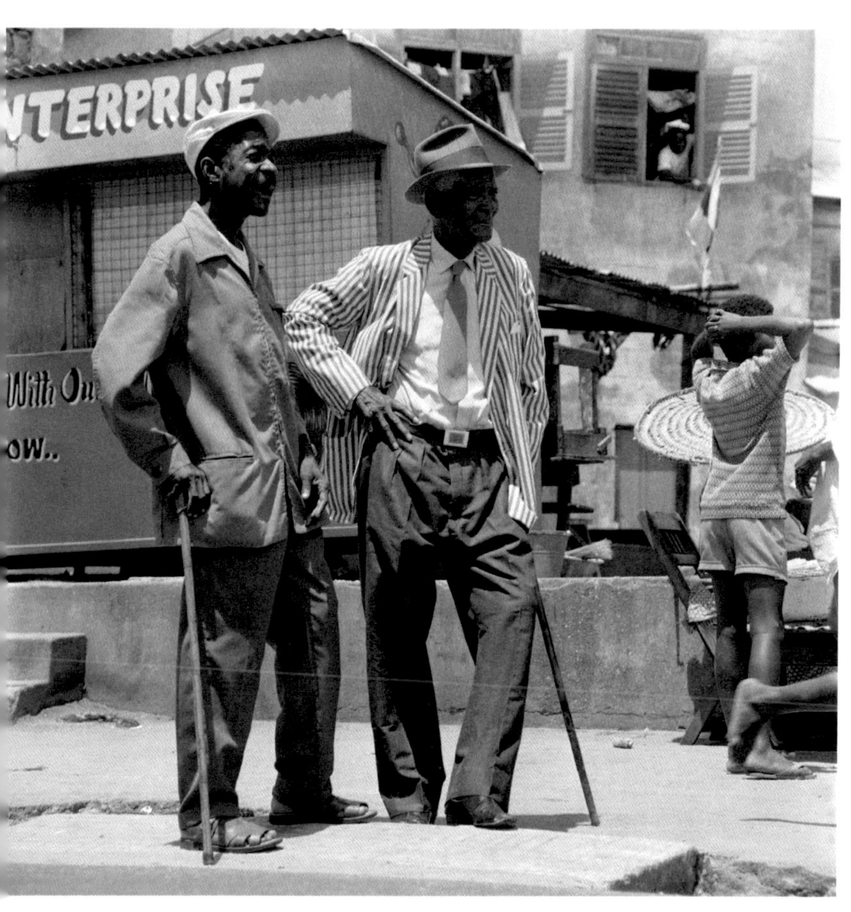

NTERPRISE
With Ou
ow..

53. Photographer Felicia Abban outside
Holy Trinity Cathedral, Accra, late 1970s.

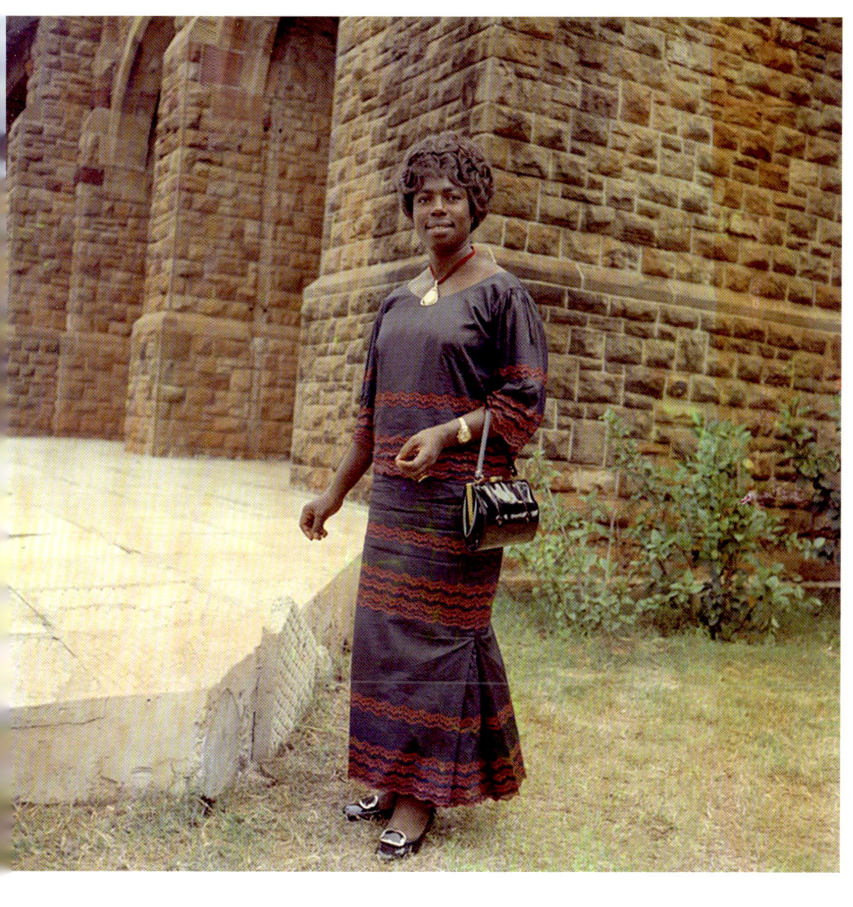

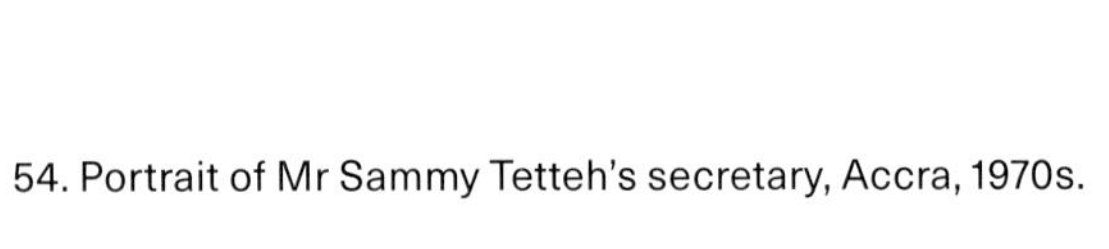

54. Portrait of Mr Sammy Tetteh's secretary, Accra, 1970s.

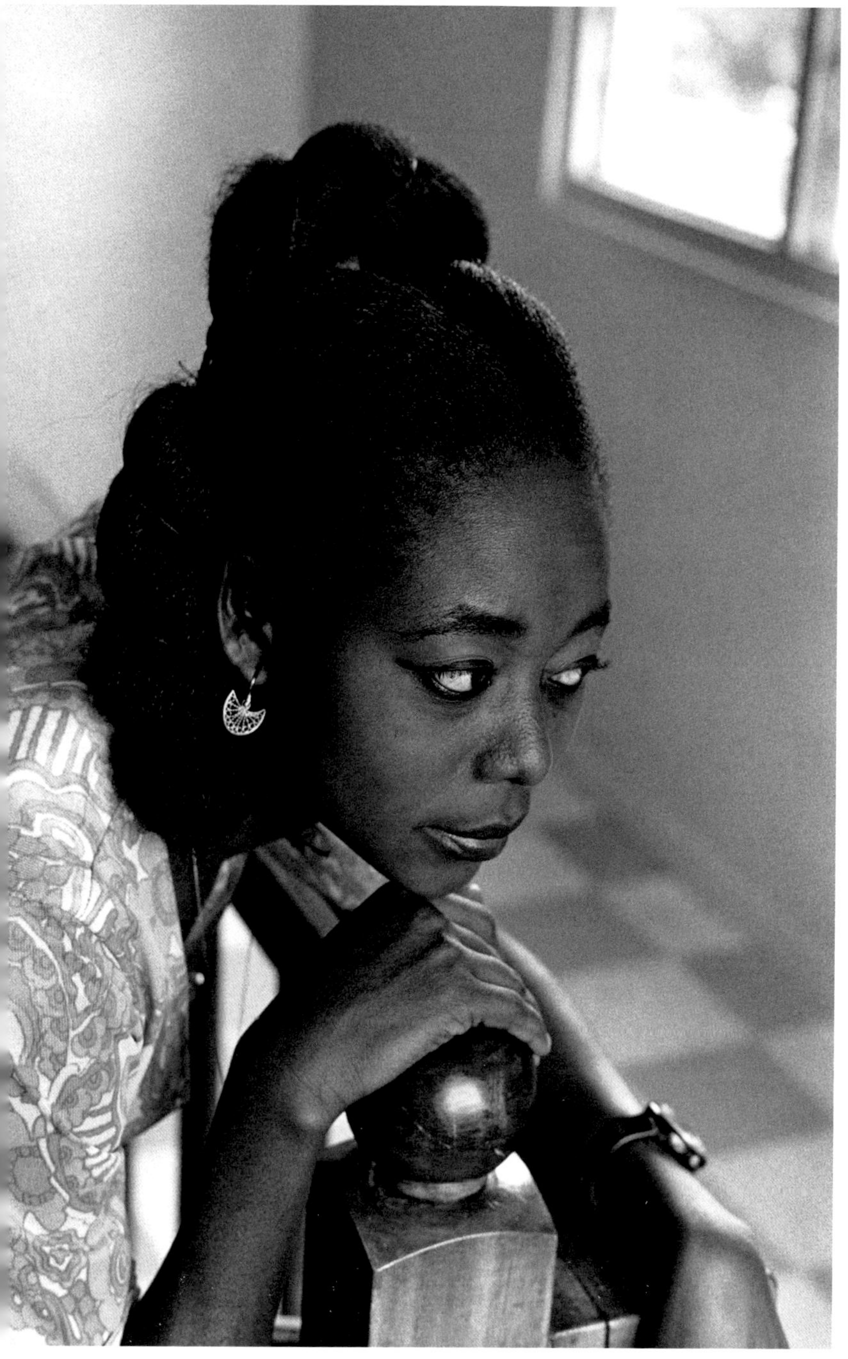

55. Margaret Obiri-Yeboah, a friend of James Barnor,
outside the Sick-Hagemeyer store, Accra, c. 1972.

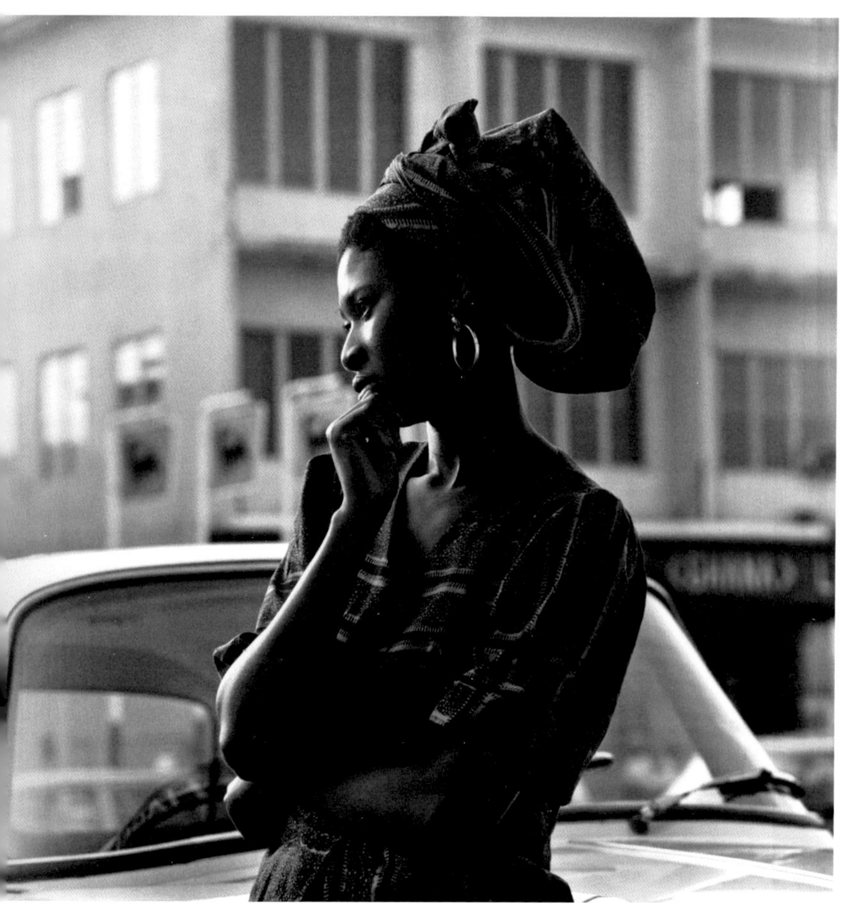

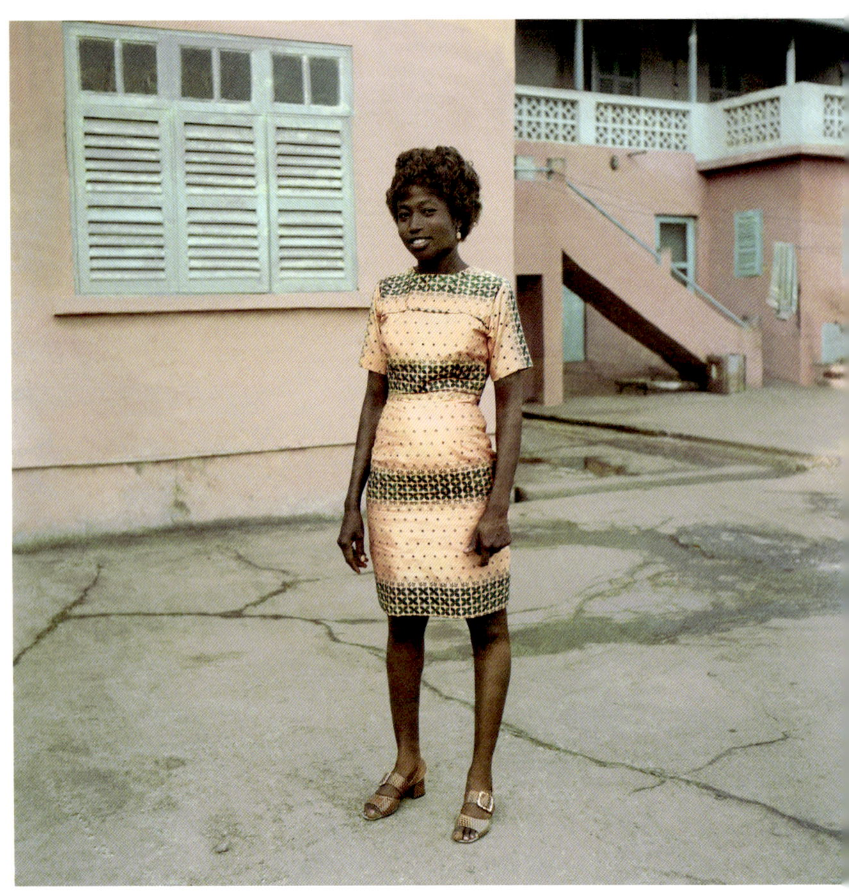

56. A relative of James Barnor's landlady in the
courtyard of their shared home, Tip Toe area,
Kokomlemle, Accra, Accra, c. 1971.

57. Sister Agoe at Studio X23, c. 1972.

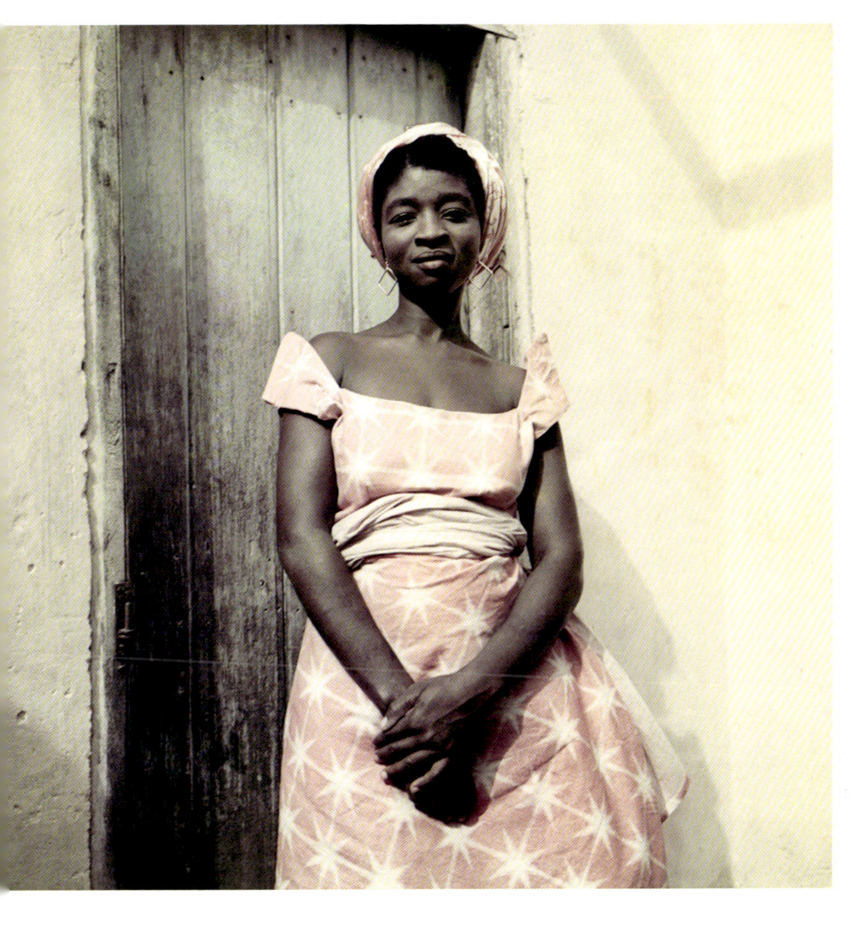

58. Filling up the Studio X23 car at the Agip petrol station
for the Agip 1974 calendar, Accra, 1973.

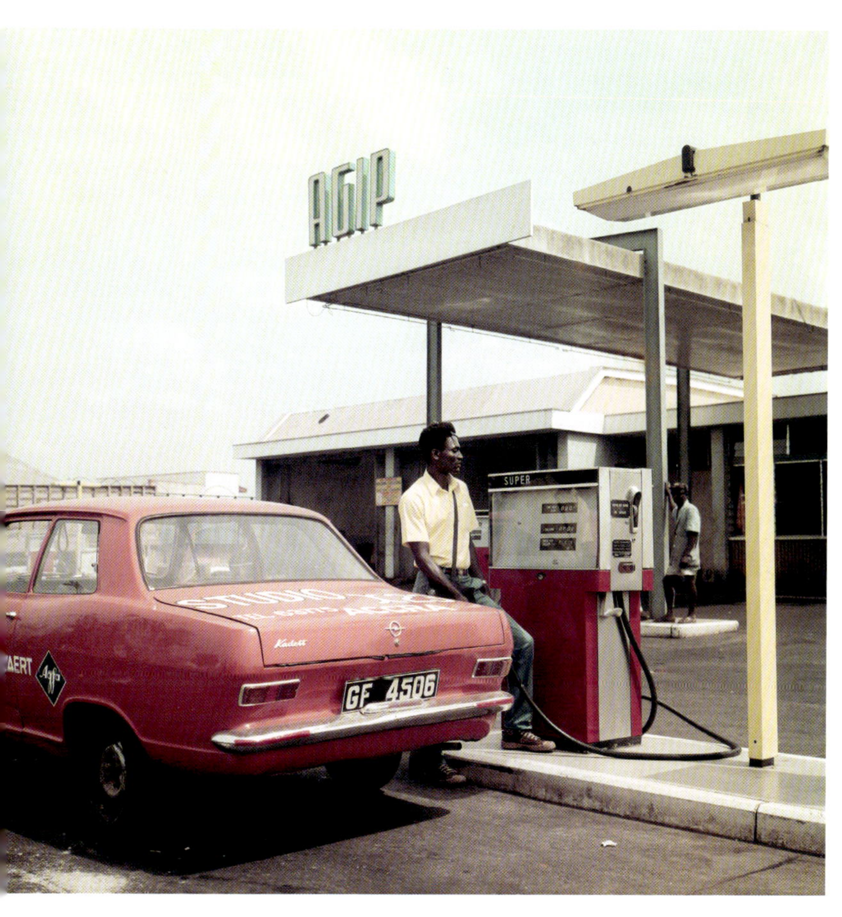

AGIP
SUPER
STUDIO
AERT
Agip
GF 4506
Kadett

59. View of a railway yard for the
1974 Agip calendar, Accra, 1973.

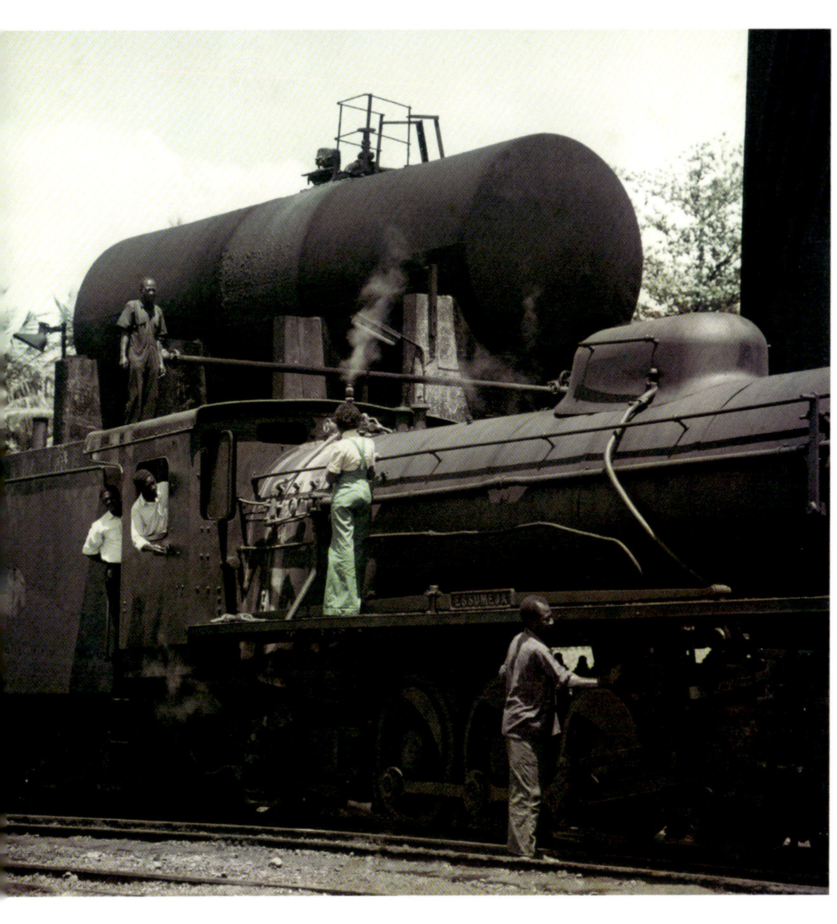

60. A model posing for the
1974 Agip calendar, Accra, 1973.

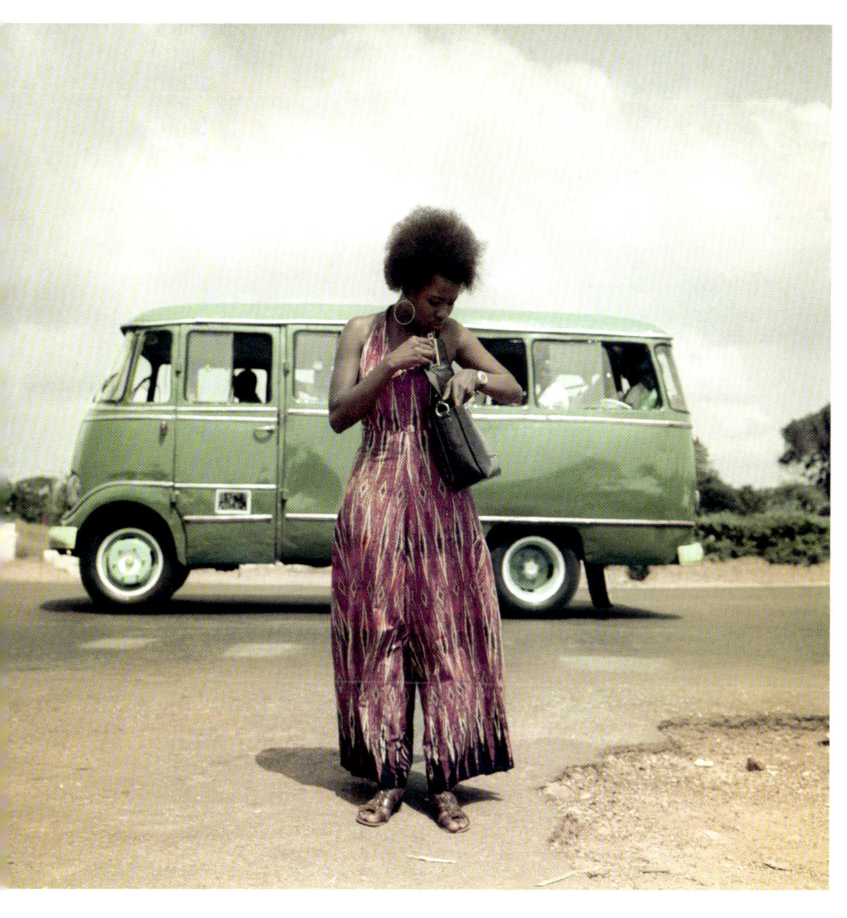

61. Sick-Hagemeyer shop assistant outside the
United Trading Company headquarters, Accra, 1971.

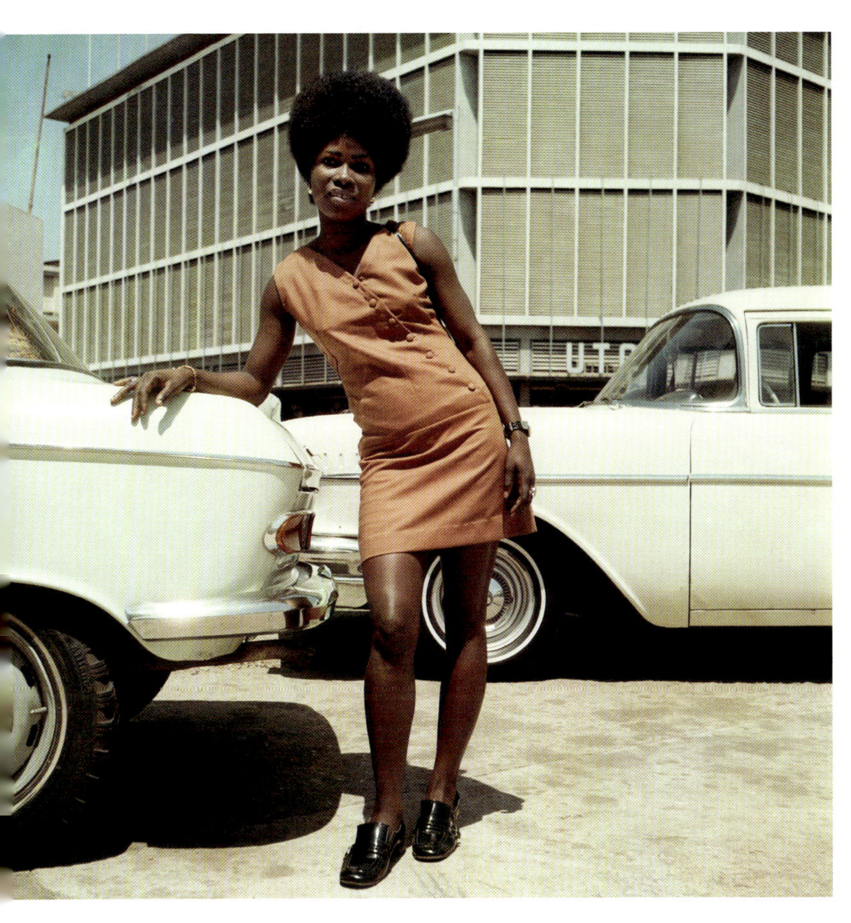

62. Publicity shot for the Roll Boy printer, Accra, 1971.

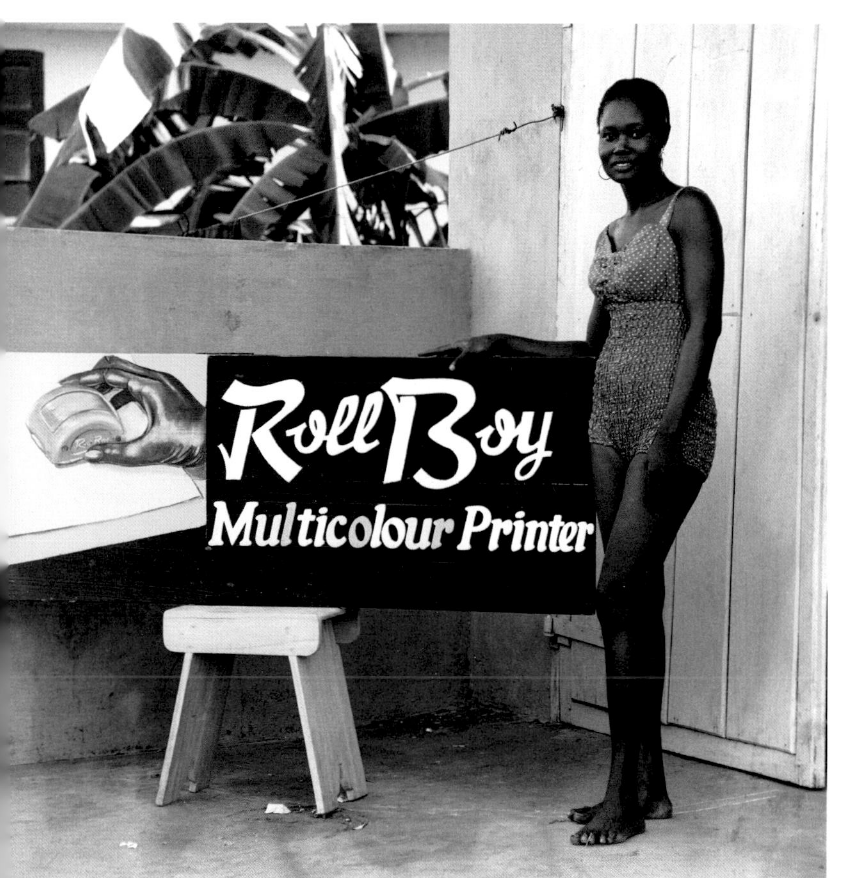
Roll Boy
Multicolour Printer

63. Sophia Salomon with two white dolls,
Tip Toe area, Kokomlemle, Accra, c. 1971–72.

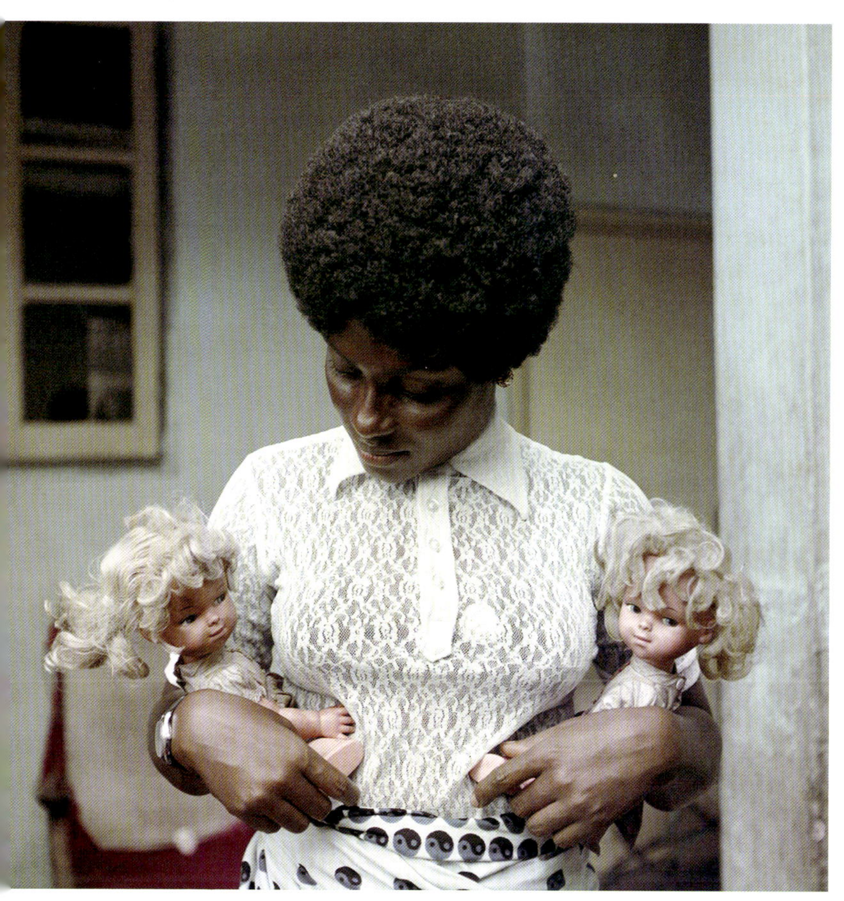

64. Little girl on the last day of Ramadan,
Tip Toe area, Kokomlemle, Accra, c. 1973.

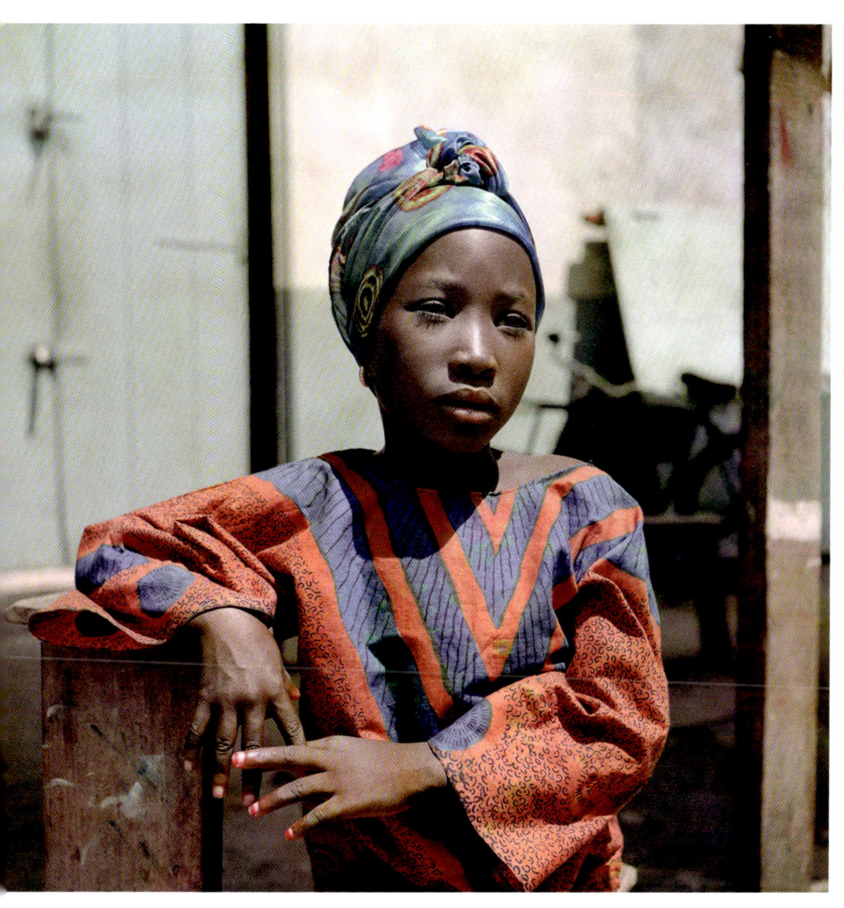

65. Little boy in his sister's arms, Accra, 1979.

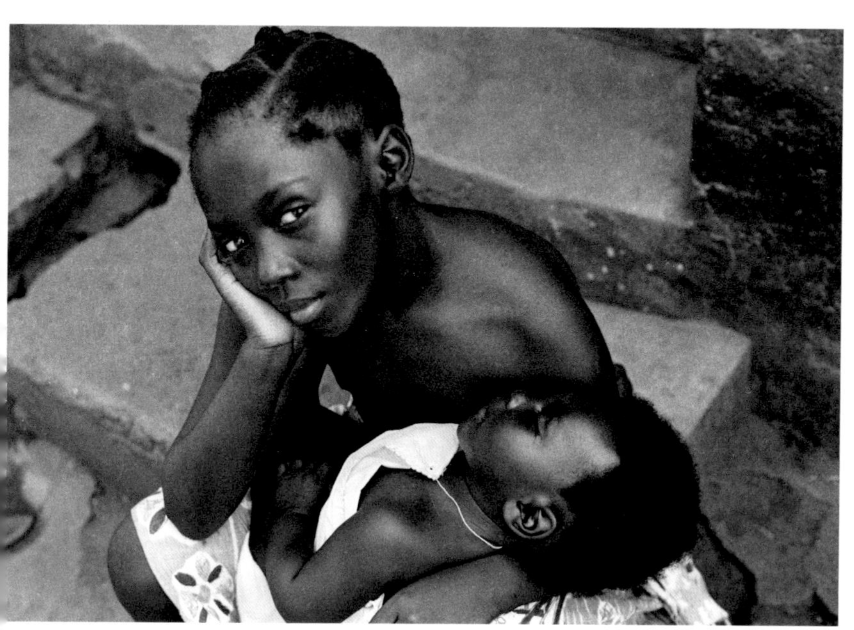

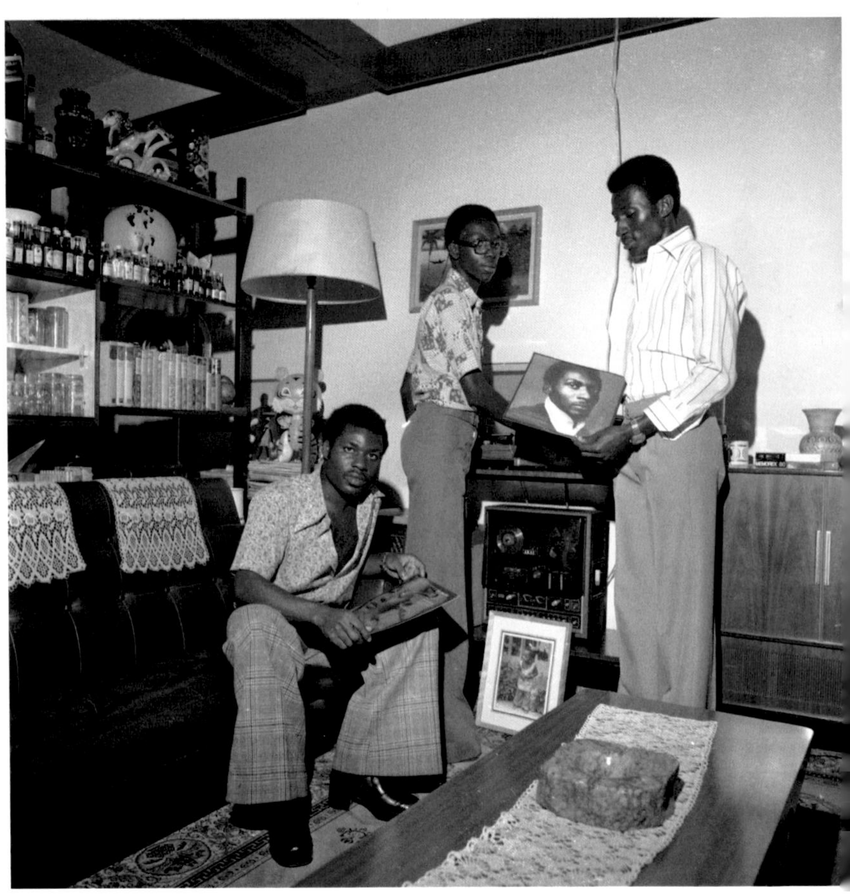

66. Quentin Quartey's house, Accra, 1970s.

67. A talented young musician from the highlife scene
who died before his career took off, Studio X23, 1977.

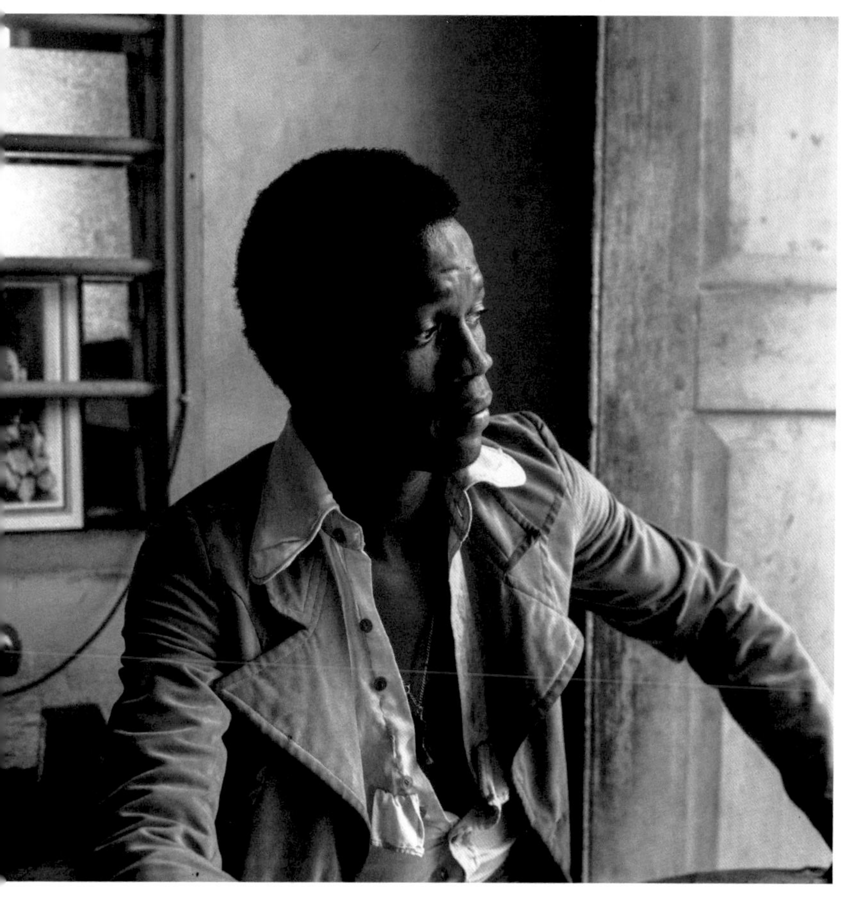

68. The members of the Youngsters Band posing for a record cover
in front of a map of Africa, Old Polo Grounds, Accra, c. 1975–76.

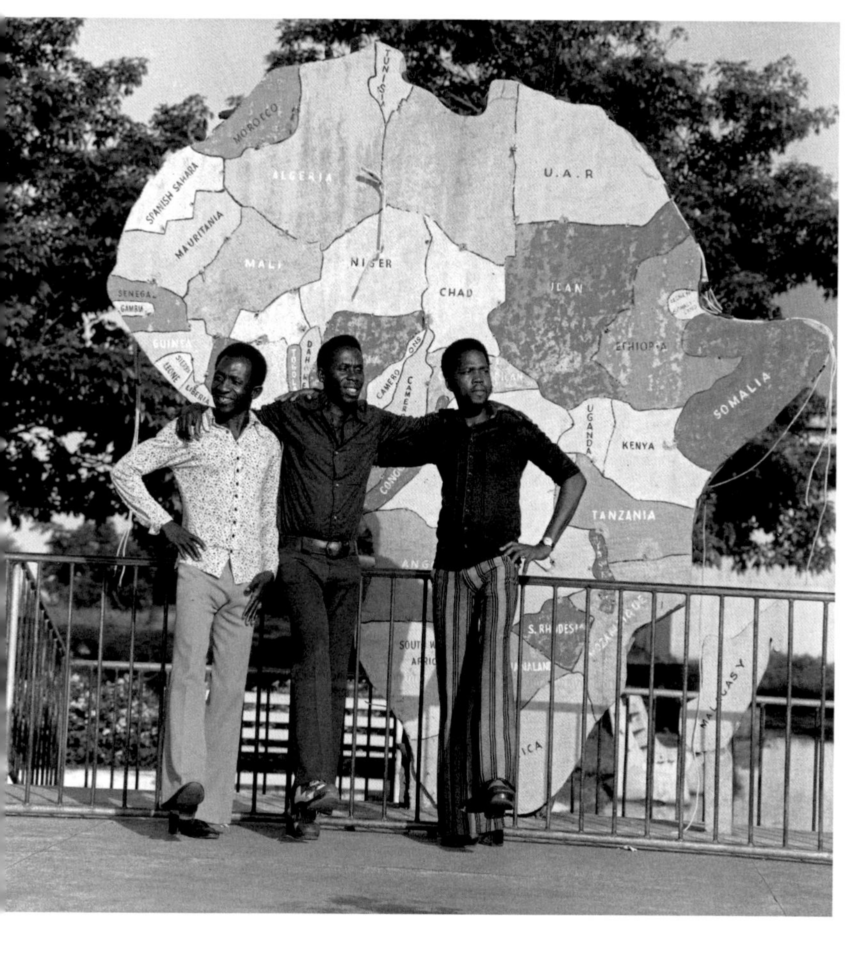

MOROCCO
TUNISIA
SPANISH SAHARA
ALGERIA
U.A.R
MAURITANIA
MALI
NIGER
CHAD
SUDAN
SENEGAL
GAMBIA
GUINEA
SIERRA
LEONE
LIBERIA
TOGO
DAHOMEY
CAMEROONS
CAMEROONS
ETHIOPIA
SOMALIA
CONGO
UGANDA
KENYA
TANZANIA
ANGOLA
SOUTH W
AFRICA
S. RHODESIA
MOZAMBIQUE
MALAGASY

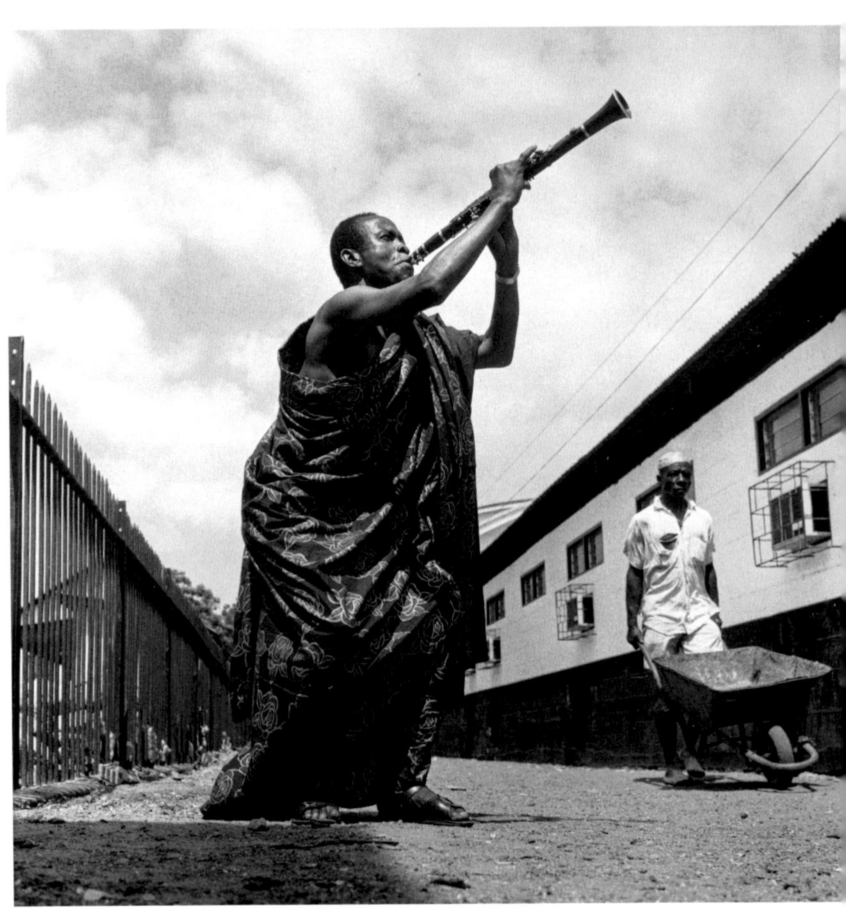

69. E.K. Nyame, the legendary Ghanaian musician, photographed for a record cover, Accra, c. 1975.

70. Fee Hi Cultural Group, performance for American musicians visiting Ghana, Studio X23, c. 1987.

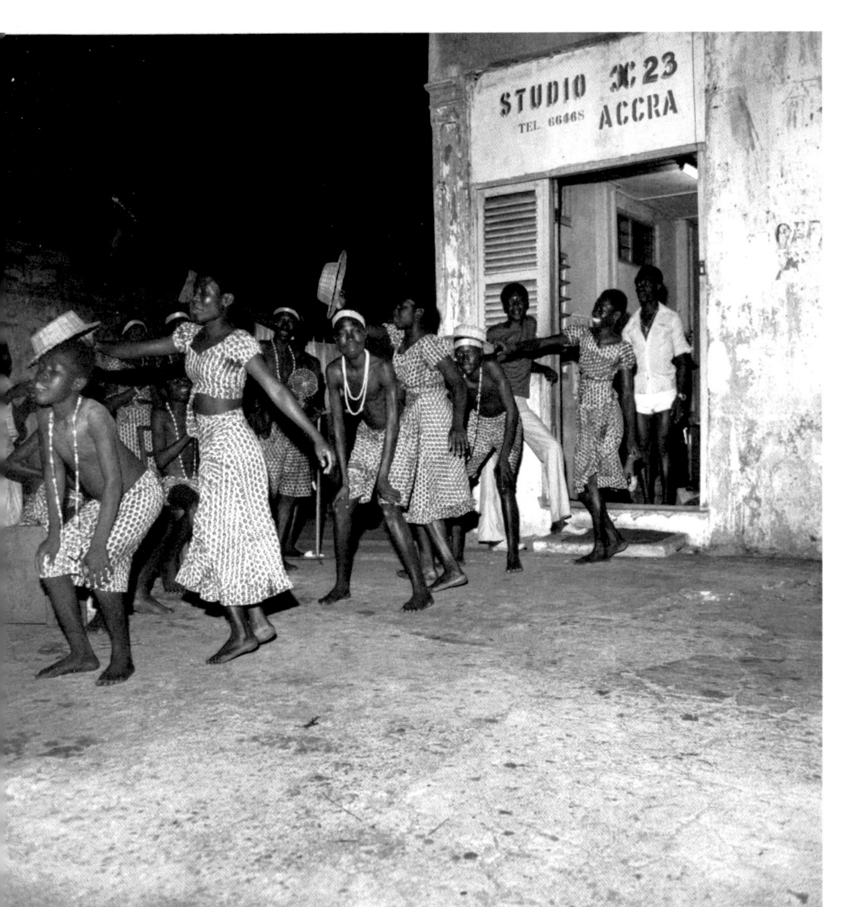

STUDIO 23
TEL. 6646S
ACCRA

71. Printmaking in the darkroom, Studio X23, c. 1983.

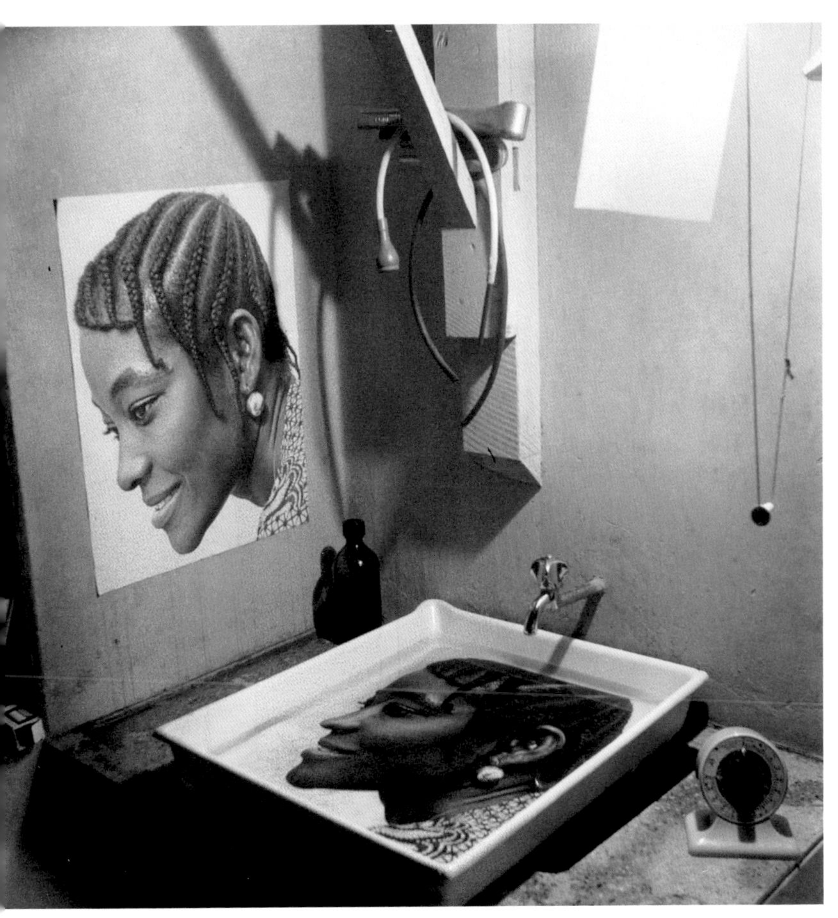

72. James Barnor's studio assistant stepping out of
the darkroom, Studio X23, between 1983 and 1987.

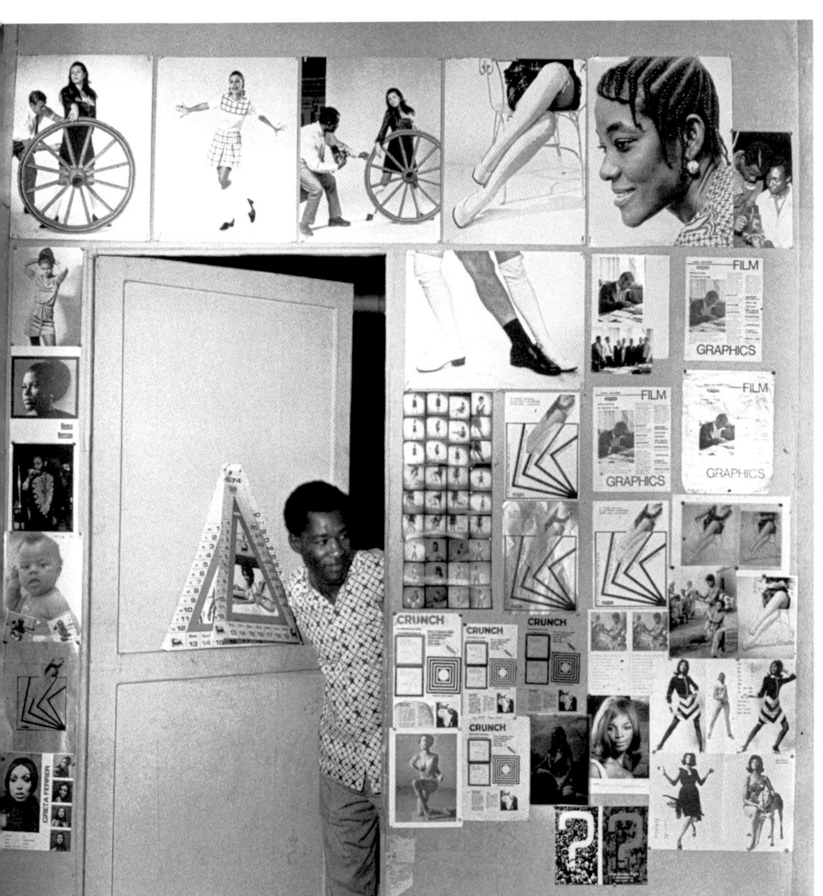

Biography

1929 Frederick Seton James Barnor is born on
6 June in Accra, in the Gold Coast (present-
day Ghana).

1945 Barnor graduates from Bishop's Boys
School in Accra and starts working as an
art teacher at St Mary's Parish School.
Kwame Nkrumah and George Padmore
organize the Fifth Pan-African Congress,
in Manchester. The delegates commit to
fighting for autonomy and independence
for colonized countries.

1947 Barnor begins a two-year apprenticeship
at Yehowa Aakwe Studio, working under
J.P. Dodoo, a renowned Accra-based portrait
photographer.
Nkrumah returns to the Gold Coast from
England to lead the political movement
calling for independence.

1948 The British Nationality Act grants all
citizens of the Commonwealth the right
to enter and live in British territory.

1949 Barnor begins his career as a
photographer by opening an outdoor studio
in the district of Jamestown in Accra.

1950 The newspaper *The Daily Graphic* is
established in Accra, funded by the British
Daily Mirror Group. Barnor is the first local
photojournalist to be hired by the *Daily
Graphic*.

1951 In February, he photographs Kwame
Nkrumah on his release from prison.
Nkrumah was imprisoned in 1950 for
inciting civil disobedience.
Drum magazine is launched in Johannesburg,
with offices throughout Africa and in London.

1952 Barnor starts working for *Drum* magazine.

1953 Barnor opens his Ever Young Studio in
the district of Jamestown in Accra.

1957 The Gold Coast gains independence and
changes its name to Ghana.
Working as a foreign correspondent,
Barnor is given accreditation to cover
the independence celebrations.

1959 Barnor moves to the UK to study
photography and improve his technical skills.

1960 He takes evening classes in photography
at the London College of Printing and learns
about colour photography by working at the
Colour Processing Laboratories (CPL) in Kent.
He then begins studying at Medway College
of Art in Rochester.

1963 Barnor finishes his studies at Medway
College of Art and starts working as a
technical assistant there. He organizes an
exhibition of Ghanaian art at the college.

1966 Barnor's first cover shot for Drum
is published in London. He works as a
photographer at the Centre of Educational
Television Overseas (CETO), as well as
the London-based advertising agency
Campbell-Drayton.
The political instability in Ghana intensifies,
leading to a coup in which Nkrumah is
deposed.

1967 Barnor continues to work as a freelance
photographer for *Drum* and is employed
as a colour printing technician at CPL in
Edenbridge.

1969 Barnor returns to Ghana after training
at Agfa-Gevaert in Germany and Belgium.

1970–73 He works as a manager for Sick-
Hagemeyer and opens the first colour
photography lab in Ghana.

1973 He opens Studio X23 in Accra.

1977–84 He is employed as a photographer
by the United States Embassy in Ghana.

1983–87 He becomes an official photographer
to the Ghanaian government, based at
Osu Castle in Accra.

1980s Barnor's studio faces a dip in demand
with the arrival of digital photography.
The artist pursues his passion for music by
becoming director of Ebaa Hi Gbiko (later
renamed Fee Hi), a group encouraging
children to be involved with cultural activities.

1983 He accompanies Ebaa Hi Gbiko on a
tour of Italy.

1987 He stops working as an official
government photographer but continues
his work with Studio X23 until 1992.

1994 He returns to the UK, living first in London, then in Kent. He brings with him all his negatives, prints, glass plates and other archive material.

1994–96 After a long period when his immigration status was unclear, he is granted indefinite leave to remain in the UK.

1996 He moves to his current home in Brentford, West London.

2010 He is contacted by Autograph ABP in London, who begin exploring his archives and digitize a selection of around a hundred images. These photographs are shown around the world in an exhibition called 'Ever Young'.

2016 After publishing a book based on the Autograph ABP collection, the Galerie Clémentine de la Féronnière sets about cataloguing and digitizing James Barnor's archive in its entirety. He begins a series of residencies at the International City of Arts in Paris, to carry out the work of captioning and documenting his photographs.

2020 He sets up the James Barnor Foundation in the UK. Dedicated to preserving his legacy, the foundation aims to advocate for the preservation and visibility of African cultures, and to support the education, training and development of African talents.

2022 Establishment of the James Barnor Prize, annually awarded to a photographer from Africa or the diaspora.

Selected Bibliography

James Barnor: Ever Young, text by Margaret
Busby and Francis Hodgson, Paris:
Clémentine de la Féronnière; London:
Autograph ABP, 2015

James Barnor: The Roadmaker, text by
Damarice Amao, Paris: Maison CF; Bristol:
RRB Photobooks, 2021

James Barnor: Accra/London – A Retrospective,
text by Lizzie Carey-Thomas and Joseph
Constable, Cologne: Walther König;
London: Serpentine Galleries, 2021

James Barnor, Stories: The Portfolio 1947–1987,
text by Damarice Amao, Clémentine de la
Féronnière, Matthieu Humery, Margaux
Lavernhe, Bianca Manu, Hans Ulrich
Obrist, Isabella Seniuta, Paris: Maison
CF; Arles: Fondation Luma; Bristol:
RRB Publishing, 2022

Selected Exhibitions

Solo exhibitions

2004 Acton Arts Festival, Acton Arts Forum, London.

2005 *James Barnor's Diaries*, Paul Robeson Theatre, Hounslow.

2007 *Mr Barnor's Independence Diaries*, Black Cultural Archives, London.

2010–16 *Ever Young: James Barnor*, Autograph ABP, London; W.E.B. Du Bois Research Institute, Harvard University, Cambridge, MA; Iziko South African National Gallery, Cape Town; Impressions Gallery, York; Galerie Clémentine de la Féronnière, Paris; Band Gallery, Toronto.

2017 *Ever Young*, Musée du Quai Branly, Paris.

2017–22 *La Vie selon James Barnor/Life According to James Barnor*, 10e Biennale des Rencontres, Bamako, Mali; Musée de la Photographie, Saint-Louis, Senegal; Gallery 1957, Accra; Gerard Sekoto Gallery, Johannesburg; CCF, Windhoek, Namibia; Alliance Française, Lusaka, Zambia; Alliance Française, Gaborone, Botswana.

2019–20 *James Barnor: A Retrospective*, Nubuke Foundation, Accra.

2021–23 *James Barnor: Accra/London – A Retrospective*, Serpentine North Gallery, London; Museo d'Arte della Svizzera Italiana, Lugano; Detroit Institute of Arts, Detroit.

2022 *James Barnor: Stories. Le portfolio 1947–1987*, Fondation Luma, Les Rencontres d'Arles.

Group exhibitions

2012 *Another London*, Tate Britain, London.

2015 *Work, Rest and Play: British Photography from the 1960s to Today*, Shanghai Misheng Art Museum.

Swinging Sixties London: Photography in the Capital of Cool, Foam, Amsterdam.

Staying Power: Photographs of Black British Experience, 1950s–1990s, Victoria & Albert Museum, London.

2018 *This Synthetic Moment*, David Nolan Gallery, New York.

It's Great to Be Young: James Barnor et Marc Riboud, Galerie Clémentine de la Féronnière, Paris.

2019 *Paris–London. Music Migrations (1962–1989)*, Musée National de l'Histoire de l'Immigration, Paris.

2019–20 *20 ans. Les acquisitions du musée du quai Branly – Jacques-Chirac*, Musée du Quai Branly – Jacques-Chirac, Paris.

2021 *Todd Webb in Africa: Outside the Frame*, Minneapolis Institute of Art; Portland Museum of Art, 2023.

2022 Africa Fashion, Victoria & Albert Museum, London.

The Photofile series is the original English-language edition of the Photo Poche collection. It was first published between 1986 and 1992 by the Centre National de la Photographie, Paris, with the support of the French Ministry of Culture. Robert Delpire (1926–2017) was the creator of the series and its managing editor until 2017.

General editors: Géraldine Lay and Christine Barthe, with the collaboration of the Galerie Clémentine de la Féronnière

Series design by Matthew Young

Translated from the French by Bethany Wright

First published in the United Kingdom in 2023 by Thames & Hudson Ltd, 181A High Holborn, London WC1V 7QX

First published in the United States of America in 2023 by Thames & Hudson Inc., 500 Fifth Avenue, New York, New York 10110

British Library Cataloguing-in-Publication Data
A catalogue record for this book is available from the British Library

Library of Congress Catalog Card Number 2023939256

ISBN: 978-0-500-29787-2

Printed and bound in Italy

Be the first to know about our new releases, exclusive content and author events by visiting
thamesandhudson.com
thamesandhudsonusa.com
thamesandhudson.com.au